Zen and the Art of Funk Capitalism

Zen and the Art of Funk Capitalism

A General Theory of Fallibility

Karun Philip

Writer's Showcase

San Jose New York Lincoln Shanghai

ZEN AND THE ART OF FUNK CAPITALISM
A GENERAL THEORY OF FALLIBILITY

iUniverse books may be ordered through booksellers or by contacting:

Writer's Showcasean imprint of iUniverse, Inc.

iUniverse
1663 Liberty Drive
Bloomington, IN 47403
www.iuniverse.com
1-800-Authors (1-800-288-4677)

Because of the dynamic nature of the Internet, any web addresses or links contained in this book may have changed since publication and may no longer be valid. The views expressed in this work are solely those of the author and do not necessarily reflect the views of the publisher, and the publisher hereby disclaims any responsibility for them.

Any people depicted in stock imagery provided by Getty Images are models, and such images are being used for illustrative purposes only.
Certain stock imagery © Getty Images.

ISBN: 978-0-5952-0514-1 (sc)

Print information available on the last page.

iUniverse rev. date: 11/25/2019

CONTENTS

FOREWORD

"Funk is the underside of anything, of everything," explains Patricia Smith, a noted 'slam' poet in Boston. In this book I explain what I have learnt, or at least what I think I have learnt, while being an entrepreneur over the last eight years. Being an academic by training, I spent my entrepreneurial years constantly comparing theoretical economics with the actual reality of the experience. What I discovered could only be termed 'Funk Capitalism,' in the spirit of Ms. Smith's definition above. In the tradition of Robert Pirsig's book 'Zen and the Art of Motorcycle Maintenance', I try to demystify philosophical 'knowledge problems' while at the same time talking about practical issues of entrepreneurship and the economy, with the intention of providing a model for economic development.

After socialism's proven failure, the last decade has been spent trying to implement capitalism through central planning in countries that are attempting to reform. But the spectacular failure of this in Russia and struggling attempts of other countries suggest that free market economists don't really know how or why capitalism works in their countries, or at least not well enough to re-create the success elsewhere.

The answer, I believe, lies in the work of Austrian economist and Nobel Laureate Friedrich August Hayek (1899–1992), who was pretty much marginalized by the economics community in the century in which he lived. Hayek is dismissed as a laissez-faire economist by the left, and as 'too liberal' by the right, and is therefore left without a constituency. In actual fact, his work shows how the concerns of the left can be addressed while retaining the efficiency that free markets can provide—he was the quintessential free-market leftist, if such a phrase can be concocted. In this set of essays, I attempt to re-state Hayek's ideas in a compact and coherent logical framework. I then use the same conceptual framework to examine issues of contemporary importance in development economics in order to arrive at a potential solution to economics' greatest problem—poverty.

The discussion covers education, enterprise, banking, intellectual property and law. In particular, I introduce a modern "new economy" analysis of the task of entrepreneurship in a globalized and automated world, and how this applies to developing economies. I cover many seminal entrepreneurial issues where I found reality at odds with what is typically taught, including marketing, branding, financing, and managing an enterprise. The full impact of this work then, is to propose a system that could almost guarantee economic growth and development in under-developed regions of the world.

The theses are made around an assumption of fallibility of knowledge, which can be seen to underlie all of Hayek's work. To be formally complete, I begin with a chapter on epistemology, discussing the philosophical issues involved with this theory of knowledge. Those not interested in philosophy can comfortably skip that chapter as long as they are willing to accept the fairly obvious assumption that our knowledge is fallible, i.e. that we can be wrong.

Some of the early reviewers of this book have been skeptical about emphasizing the importance of fallibility because it seems I am telling the reader that there is nothing to believe in. But in fact, the opposite is true. In the book I discuss why I believe in data, I believe in evidence, I believe in presumption of innocence in a trial, I believe in due process of law, I believe in democracy, I believe in individual liberty, I believe that it is wrong for individuals to coerce other individuals, and I believe in the power of banking and capital, used without coercion or favor, to completely eliminate poverty forever. The following pages describe why I believe all these follow from the assumption of the fallibility of knowledge.

EPISTEMOLOGY

This book is intended to state certain theories that appear to explain more than prevailing theories explain—in other words, it purports to tell the story of what is true of the universe in which we live. If we are to tell the story of what is true, we must then begin with an investigation of what constitutes valid knowledge and what does not. Indeed, what do we mean by the word "knowledge"? The field of science concerned with this question is called epistemology, and this is what we must begin with.

The role of language

Since the knowledge I strive to express in this book is expressed in language, i.e. in words, we must first understand the relationship between words, our minds, and the material universe. If we listen to the biologists, our brains consist of neurons that are interconnected in complex ways that we do not fully comprehend as yet. But even the simplest artificial simulation of neural interactions shows the ability of neural networks to classify perceptions. It seems congruent with our psychological experience to see that our minds do, in fact, perform this task. We perceive the external universe and all our perception is essentially the perception of difference. Blue is different from red. Water is different from sand. Dogs are different from cats. Because of the perceived difference, we come up with different words to address and communicate the perceived difference. The act of perception of difference therefore naturally yields the development of words and language.

Of course, with each perception of difference, there is an implied collectivization of similarity. By perceiving dogs and cats as different, we are effectively perceiving all cats to be similar to each other. Of course it is important to note that the similarity does not imply exact sameness. In fact within any collectivized category, we can find further differentiation. The material universe seems infinitely differentiated, and even after going down to sub-atomic levels we are unable to find any entity that cannot be perceived as divisible further or differently.

Aristotle's syllogism

Much of epistemology works by separating the world of material objects from the world of words. When we take words that we initially created to signify perceived differences, and remove the content from them, we can construct general sentences that might apply to different real objects or situations. For instance, we can perceive that birds fly and also that leaves fly in the wind. From that we can abstract that things fly under certain circumstances, and perhaps develop theories about wind and air. Aristotle was one great thinker who managed to develop the theory of logic by explaining this process of abstraction. His work produced the basic tool of epistemology, called a syllogism. A syllogism basically states that if we have one statement that says "If A then B" and another statement that says "If B then C" then we can construct a third statement "If A then C" that must be true if the first two statements are true. Of course, when we apply this theory back to real objects and events, we must add a caveat. For instance, we can state "assuming no unforeseen facts, if fire causes smoke, and if smoke causes pollution, then fire causes pollution". But we can never leave out the "assume no unforeseen facts" because the certainty of the conclusion depends on the assumption that the underlying statements are true. This clause is sometimes called the "ceteris paribus" clause after its Latin root.

Epistemology vs. ontology

Of course, to state that the law of syllogism exists separately from the material universe seems ridiculous. It is a sentence that is constructed by and resident in our brains, our neurons, all which are all part of the material universe. Nevertheless, there is a perceivable difference between the world of thoughts and the world of material things excluding thoughts, so it is not unreasonable that we assign different words to the two realms. One world, commonly called the "real world" consists of words assigned to material objects that we perceive, excluding words themselves—or what we might call first-order words. The other world, the "mental universe" consists of the first-order words themselves as well as words assigned to different aspects of the words themselves, or "higher-order words". Both these worlds are represented by mental constructs in our brains but we refer to one as the real world and the other as the mental world. The study of this "real world" is referred to as ontology and the study of the "mental world" is referred to as epistemology.

Paradigm shifts and fallibility

Going back to the Aristotelian syllogism now, many Aristotelians claim that the use of the method of syllogism provides "apodictic certainty" or demonstrable certainty that certain knowledge is true even if has not been perceived already. For instance, an Aristotelian might claim that Newton's laws of gravity are true and will always remain true because they follow the scientifically formal method of syllogistic theory. Now it is historically true that after Newton's laws were discovered, we have been able to predict much more of the material universe than we were able to prove earlier. But

Einstein showed that the laws break down when we approach speeds near that of the speed of light. What then of apodictic certainty? Well, if you go back to Aristotle, you can clearly see that it is dependent on the "ceteris paribus" clause. If there is some axiom that we have implicitly assumed, and then if we apply the theory in a place where that axiom is not true, then our all-powerful "law" may become invalid. Knowledge gained through the use of syllogism is therefore not infallible when applied to real situations. This fact has become increasingly widely accepted since the work of Thomas Kuhn who showed that such paradigm shifts occur periodically in science where old views are overthrown by new views, often when an important implicit assumption is unmasked. The key to understanding this is to realize that these laws are merely sentences we construct mentally using language. The sentences seek to explain phenomena we perceive, but they will always be fallible statements, at least because they are necessarily incomplete. To say that the law of gravity is fallible does not mean that the perceived phenomena currently thought of as due to gravity do not occur. Simply that some future theory, such as quantum mechanics, may explain that phenomenon much better and in a more complete fashion, and the way we think of gravity today may be dropped completely. Instead of believing that the material universe follows certain laws, we should instead believe that the material universe behaves in ways that are well approximated by the laws (statements) we invent. Science is the enterprise of constantly seeking better approximations of the way the material universe behaves.

Gödel: proving fallibility

The fallibility of knowledge would not be proven as important as a concept if it wasn't for the work of Kurt Gödel, especially as explained by J. R. Lucas. Gödel showed that no matter what set of axioms you choose, even in a completely imaginary mathematical universe, there could always be a sentence that you could construct that could not be proven either true or false. This implies that no set of axioms can be complete *even in an imaginary world where the "inconvenience" of material reality is excluded*!! If we are guaranteed that all sets of axioms are incomplete, then we can prove that all theories, i.e. all applications of syllogism, are fallible. So Gödel's proof of incompleteness is equivalently a proof of necessary fallibility of knowledge, as Lucas points out.

The implications of this are revolutionary, as Lucas realized. Of course, we all know from day to day experience that our knowledge is fallible. We have certain expectations, and sometimes they don't get met. We try to plan to correct for fallible expectations, but we are never able to achieve perfect results. Most of the time we assume the mistake was ours and could have been prevented if only we had a little more knowledge. Yet epistemological investigations ending with Gödel tell us the truth is that ALL our knowledge is fallible, and inevitably so! In fact, according to Ludwig Wittgenstein, we cannot even assert that the material universe is real or that what we perceive in the room is actually there. At one meeting, Bertrand Russell was unable to convince Wittgenstein that there they could be *certain* there was no rhinoceros in the room with them!

Ramanuja: dealing with fallibility

One of the most elegant ways of extricating ourselves from this mess of provable fallibility is provided by an 11th century Indian philosopher by the name of Ramanuja. Now, ancient Indian philosophy, rediscovered around 800 AD by the philosopher Sankara and termed as "Advaita" or "non-dualist" philosophy, has always maintained that all knowledge is fallible. But typically, the interpretation has been made that the material universe is not necessarily real, resulting in a beautiful but sometimes incomprehensible diversity of spiritual life in India. While it is histori-cally certain that this outlook on life brings great cultural diversity and is conducive to peaceful coexistence, it leaves a modern science-influenced mind somewhat unsatisfied. The elegant answer is not, however, to be found in Western philosophy, but in Ramanuja's theory of Visista Advaita or "special theory of non-dualism". According to Ramanuja, even though all knowledge is fallible, as propounded by virtually all schools of Advaita, we must ASSUME the material universe exists and is real—we must take it as an article of faith despite having no claim to infallible knowledge. "Maya" or the illusion of reality created by our minds should not be interpreted to suggest that reality is an illusion, rather only that our individual understanding of reality is fallible. Ramanuja's philosophy suggests that objective Science is possible—that we can continually study the material universe and discover better and better understandings of it, even though we will never have an infallible or complete understanding of it. According to Ramanuja, and congruent with the work done by Karl Popper in the West almost a thousand years later, criticism of existing theories is the precise methodology by which we can arrive at ever better understanding. Even the sacred book of the Vedas, which are considered the source of Indian philosophy, can be misunderstood, Ramanuja claimed. To arrive at the correct meaning, one would have to continually criticize ones own understanding of the words until one arrived at an understanding that stood up to criticism. For Ramanuja, who was also religious in the traditional sense, the word 'God' is defined by saying "the material universe is the body of God". So God/Nature is to be discovered by man using reason and science, revealed little by little, but never ever known completely or infallibly. So while objectivity through critical rationalism is a methodology to hopefully reveal or discover more and more of reality, the Advaitin maxim of the fallibility of all knowledge will always continue to hold. In Ramanuja and Popper then, we find the precise point at which Eastern and Western philosophies find common ground.

Hayek's Axiom

So why do I refer to the theory that "all knowledge, when expressed in language, is fallible" as Hayek's Axiom? Well, knowledge of fallibility seems to be as old as civilization itself. The ancient Indians knew of it. The greatest of Greek philosophers, Socrates, spoke essentially of the fallibility of human knowledge. Certainly, all major world religions state that human knowledge is fallible. And Karl Popper did make it his life's work and along with Thomas Kuhn, laid the foundation for post-modern studies in the philosophy of science. However, in my opinion, it was not until Friedrich Hayek that all the implications of fallibility were fully explained. Hayek's fallibility also derived from incompleteness but not the epistemological incompleteness of Gödel. Hayekian incompleteness is simply an acknowledgement that there are too many facts in any economy for any individual or group to know. But the conclusion he reaches as a result of this more "ontological" incompleteness is the same—that the fallibility of knowledge is obvious. The implications to law, to government, to science, to virtually every form of human action are all laid out in all Hayek's work, though he does not explicitly use the axiom itself. In the following pages, I attempt to paraphrase Hayek's insights in various fields using the axiom of fallibility as stated above, occasionally adding further implications that become obvious once we understand this viewpoint. If we attempt to find the syllogistic deductions from the axiom of fallibility, then we may be able to come up with deductions and predictions that are accurate and can hold up to criticism for the foreseeable future.

It is important to note that fallibility does not mean falsehood—only the possibility of falsehood, along with the possibility of truth. Hayek's Axiom admits its own fallibility, but what we will attempt to do is assume it is true until and unless it can be refuted. The flip side of fallibility is possibility—there is always hope that something never previously solved can be solved because the thesis that nothing can be done is fallible. In fact, any solution to any problem almost certainly needs hope to begin with; otherwise the problem will likely not be solved. An assumption of fallibility automatically brings in such hope by ruling out any certainty in an expectation of negative outcome.

An interesting aside: since the fallibility axiom is provable through the mathematics of Gödel, it refers to a truth that belongs to all cultures that use any language, even if such cultures exist as simulation on a computer, or elsewhere in the galaxy or universe. Science Fiction stories of super-intelligent alien races or super-intelligent artificial robots therefore are proven somewhat mistaken in their imagination then, since any intelligence that was sufficiently intelligent would sooner or later discover that all knowledge is fallible. Fallibility is a cosmic speed limit on intelligence, whether artificial, human on non-human!

Competitive Discovery, Freedom, and Coercion

Engineering vs. science

In the previous section, we have effectively committed ourselves to the voluntary assumption that the material universe is real, despite the inadequate nature of our minds to verify that that happens to be infallibly true. Once done, however, science then becomes a worthwhile effort—we seek to use our fallible power of deduction to reveal more and more of how the parts of the material universe interact. At every stage, our theories will continue to be incomplete and therefore fallible, but if we can use the theory to engineer ourselves some desired outcome, then we need not be concerned by the fact that the theory is fallible and focus on the fact that it did, in fact, help us to mold the material universe in a particular way. To give a simple example, medieval Europeans assumed that the sun rises every day and planned their actions based on it. Now, even if the true fact is revealed that the earth rotates around its axis and it is technically the earth that is "falling" and not the sun that is "rising", it really does not affect the bulk of their planning and actions significantly. So fallibility of our knowledge does not seem to prevent us from muddling through life anyway—engineering is possible even if the underlying science is bad or incomplete. At the same time, better and better theories and science will help us accomplish more and more practical engineering as we reveal more accurate theories about the material universe.

Competitive epistemology

But how are we to find better and better theories if the basic methodology of syllogism itself is fallible? The answer is, and has always been, competitive theories. Since reality exists, sooner or later the less accurate theory will be shown to be incorrect and the more accurate one will prevail. For instance, we might assume for eternity that flapping our hands fast enough would help us fly, but sooner or later people who try out that theory tend to abandon it. Of course, this does not mean that flying in an airplane or hang-glider is not possible, so this does not mean we should stop trying to achieve the outcomes that are currently considered impossible—only that we should think laterally to find a solution, where the word "solution" implies the same end but not necessarily similar means.

The tool of criticism

Now, it is not strictly necessary that competitive discovery of knowledge requires more than one person. We could also use the tool of self-criticism to test our theories, as suggested by Ramanuja and Popper. But each individual goes through a unique interaction with the reality around them through their life, and each individual's theories have been shaped by actual facts of interaction in reality. So by using the competitive arguments of a large number of people, and striving to find a theory that is in conformance with the experience of all the individuals, we have a larger chance of finding the true nature of the material universe.

The act of living peacefully in a society itself, then, automatically provides a safety net against fallibility. The danger, however, is that societies can collectively believe in theories that are not, in fact, true. So it is also essential for a society to consider the theories of individuals who do not completely conform to the accepted practices of the group. Else, progress toward revealing more and more about the material universe will halt.

Tradition, freedom, consequence, and coercion

This brings us to the essential point about the choices we face individually. How far do we go as individuals to make a point about some aspect of reality that we perceive but one that has not become accepted generally in the society? We know our theory is fallible, but despite that, we also know that the generally accepted theory is also fallible. Free speech and free criticism of our speech becomes the framework under which society can continually test the limits of our knowledge.

Of course, pure thought would be useless, given fallibility. We need to act—to interact with the rest of the material universe, including other individuals—to get data that we can think about. So do we need freedom of action in order to be able to do whatever acts we feel like doing in order to discover more and more about reality? Of course we do, but given the fact that we may always be wrong, the limit of free action must be to avoid coercion of the actions of other individuals. The ever-present doubt that fallibility confers can never let us have the confidence or "justification" to use force or power to coerce another individual from acting in a particular way—after all, how do we know that that would provide the outcome we want? In fact, it is against your own interest to coerce someone else because given fallibility, you can never be sure what your own best interests are. Coercing another rather than trying to convince them would reduce the likelihood of discovering the course of action that is optimal. In the process of convincing other people about a course of actions, we may end up modifying our own theories and end up at a course of action that one would not have otherwise thought about. Convincing other people and being open to being convinced becomes an absolutely essential methodology we must use, given the fact of proven fallibility of our knowledge. Coercion would only be counter-productive.

Deriving from the axiom of fallibility this ethic that no individual should coerce any other individual turns out to be the most important and fundamental implication of fallibility. It provides us a rational definition of morality and ethics itself—we should be free to take whatever actions and speak whatever words we want to as individuals, but the point at which we must limit ourselves is coercion. Anything that involves coercing another individual must be considered immoral and unethical, and conversely anything that does not involve coercion of one individual by another individual cannot be immoral or unethical, though it may prove unsustainable or non-optimal for the individual concerned. But simply because we feel that some behavior is not going to be consistent with the nature of reality, we cannot prohibit others from trying out that behavior, as long as they do not coerce any other individual. If in fact the behavior is sustainable, that person will discover it and probably be joined by other individuals. If the behavior is not sustainable, that person will discover it for himself or herself. Experienced elders and wise people may always seek to guide their fellow community members away from behavior that will not be sustainable, but it is ultimately up to each individual to choose what course to follow, as long as it does not involve coercion of others. The resulting behaviors may indeed vary from region to region and culture to culture. Presumably, communication between cultures will allow each culture to learn from the mistakes and successes of other cultures. Morality, ethics and traditions within each culture can be specific and varied, but all cultures would need to accept the basic truth of fallibility of knowledge, and its implication that coercion is wrong. To those infallibilists who attempt to coerce us to follow some particular cultural code that they claim is the right one, we can legitimately ask why they think they are infallible in their recommendation. If they point us to a religious book, we can legitimately ask whether that book itself does not claim that all human knowledge is fallible, as do all the books of the major world religions.

However, it is worth noting again, as Hayek did, that traditions are the best defense against fallibility of knowledge, and going against them often proves to be perilous. Freedom of action means also accepting the consequences of one's actions, many of which may be unanticipated consequences that one did not want. Some of this consequence is due to basic truths about the material universe that will always be true, and some due to the fallible expectations of general society. Though expectations are fallible, people do not generally consider their expectations fallible, and when their expectations prove to be at odds with reality they may be driven to great negative emotions of fear, anger, or envy and put obstacles in the way of change. The only non-coercive way around this is step-by-step progress and taking the time and effort to show why new developments are not going to increase coercion, and when disagreements persist, to agree to disagree in peace and let time tell the truth eventually. It is important to notice that active debate and argument between people trying to convince each other of the correctness or incorrectness of their theories is an essential part of knowledge discovery and cannot be considered coercion. Free speech may hurt feelings but they can never physically constitute coercion—hurt feelings are more due to fallible expectations than anything else and such hurt diminishes once one realizes that. It may be true that the words that cause hurt can be proved to be incorrect, especially if they are stated in an infallibilist way. But given provable fallibility it is easy to discredit anyone claiming infallible knowledge. Convincing via free debate and critique is an effective alternative to coercion for everything from religious differences to moral differences to scientific discovery.

Faith & religion

The 20th century was the age of high "modernism," where rationalism turned to hubris, and religion was attacked in all its forms. It appears that attitudes toward religion in the post-modern world have tempered that hubris, as we discover that rational theories are inevitably fallible. The 21st century then is the appropriate time for us to read Hayek and understand the rational implications of fallibility without necessarily falling back to any irrational interpretations of religion, while at the same time learning what all religions have always told us regarding fallibility. It seems clear with the hindsight of the fallibility axiom, that what the major world religions essentially accomplish is to bring about peaceful interaction between people by using a concept of God to implicitly prohibit any claims to infallible knowledge. The problem with using a concept of an anthropomorphic God—a God that is similar in structure and nature to a human being—is that it allows infallibilism to persist through religious fundamentalism by interpreting religious texts in a particular way without comprehending that our understanding of words may be fallible, and indeed whoever wrote the words might have incompletely or incorrectly expressed the essential truth of fallibility that they experienced. Words may mean one thing to a writer and something somewhat different to the reader of those same words. As people communicate ideas over generations, the original meanings may get completely obscured.

But using the fallibility axiom as a core of knowledge, it becomes easier to sort through the meaning of the words of spiritual leaders and understand it in a rational way. For instance the idea of faith is often presented as something mystical in nature. But if all our knowledge is fallible due to the nature of our brain's construction and the nature of language, then it becomes quite obvious that every action of ours requires a degree of faith that what we *think* is true, *is* actually true. I think that when I put my foot forward I will meet a hard surface and enable me to walk ahead. I have no infallible claim to that knowledge, but using Ramanuja's assumption that the material world exists and my perceptions are giving me data points about this material world, I step ahead anyway in the confidence that I will walk. I do not have certainty, but I use my senses and my intellect and replace certainty with confidence. If it turns out that I step on an icy surface and fall down, this gives me further data points to ensure that in the future I attempt to perceive the difference between a dry surface and an icy surface. But at each step, all of my actions require that I have faith, confidence, in the knowledge that I consider to be true at that point in time. It would be impossible to get through life in the face of provable fallibility, without that faith. So I step ahead despite my continuing fallibility even after I have solved the ice problem because whatever is still incomplete about my newly revised theory, I can be sure that reality will teach me in due course. I need not fear stepping ahead because once I have stepped, I will get any further data points I need about reality to be able to navigate it. All I need is complete faith that the material world is real and is therefore capable of teaching me what I need in a situation it gets me to, as long as I am open to looking for data points without fear.

So why use a rational conception of faith if religious conceptions of faith are more proven and established as traditions throughout the world? Well, for one, the world is so interconnected in the 21st century that we cannot but interact with people of diverse religious backgrounds. Each religion has created a cultural context around their theology that is not completely compatible with cultures based on other theologies. What both rationalists and traditionally religious people can agree about though, is the concept of unavoidable fallibility of human knowledge. What will be more controversial is that a rational fallibilist cannot possibly accept any infallibilist claims by people claiming to be religious or political or community leaders. If we examine each religious society we will find some people that understand their religion as the source of the knowledge that all individuals are fallible. There are others who misinterpret written words in one particular way, and believe their interpretation is infallible, and then attempt to use coercion to enforce that particular view. It would be unacceptable for a rational fallibilist to accept a religious or political leader as an all-knowing dictator of all actions, and the rationale for such rejection is contained within each religion itself—the simple fact that claims of individual infallibility is heretical within the theology, i.e., all major religions already emphasize that human knowledge is fallible. If a religious person seems unreasonably fundamentalist about some issue, simply ask how he is so absolutely sure of his view, given that his own religious text tells him that human knowledge is fallible. A religious or political or community leader can be a guide so that we do not have to re-learn the facts of life from first-principles and personal discovery, but a good leader would realize that he or she does not know everything, nor indeed anything infallibly.

LAW & GOVERNMENT

The purpose of law

In the face of fallibility, the purpose of law would be to outlaw coercion. But coercion is a word that is difficult, if not impossible, to fully define so we must be reconciled to continually refine our definition of each specific type of coercion as we detect it. To begin with, physical violence against another individual is surely coercion and should be outlawed. Hayek points out that fraud is equivalent to coercion, and suggests that non-disclosure of some types of information can be construed as coercion. For Hayek, a wise society sets up government monopoly on coercion but (a) uses that coercion only to ban individuals from coercing one another, and (b) as far as possible, uses a milder form of coercion than the coercion it is outlawing or punishing. Due process of law and the assumption of innocence are the hallmarks of modern civilization, and it is easy to understand why they are necessary once we understand that knowledge is fallible, and we might inadvertently convict the wrong person. Additionally, Hayek shows that the enforcement of such a ban on coercion can be done through a decentralized system (such as the separation of the judiciary and protection of independent journalism). The ban on some forms of coercion may be even possible through private institutions, rather than a central authority trying to implement the rules that emerge through brute force. Dictatorial approaches inevitably require devolution of unlimited discretionary power to individual bureaucrats who, being fallible, inevitably use that discretionary power coercively and unjustly.

Democracy as a spontaneous detector of coercion

Although democratic forms of government historically emerged for various reasons, we can also see from the history of democratic countries that by granting political power equally to each voter, economically or socially powerless citizens who are being coerced by those more powerful than them have an opportunity to express that fact, and politicians have an incentive to use the government monopoly on coercion to redress those acts of coercion. Democracy also allows society to progress in an orderly fashion from a state in which not all coercion is banned (as is a historical fact in all nations of the world today) potentially to a state where all coercion is banned, by proceeding in a culturally sensitive step-by-step fashion so that public opinion is carried at each step. After all, if the laws that are made are not accepted in the hearts and minds of the citizens, they are of little use. Hayek describes democracy as the precise tool that forces people with good ideas to first convince other people that the ideas are good, in the process possibly modifying the ideas themselves to become less fallible and more consistent with each citizen's experience of reality. Sudden changes planned centrally and implemented without the buy-in of the people it affects can leave a social system without the safeguards needed to preempt coercive activity in the changed environment. Change undertaken under a distributed power structure such as democracy, with each participant keeping in mind that new forms of coercive activity may emerge in a changed regime, will allow private institutions to spontaneously emerge to check coercive behavior. Rather than setting up bureaucracies, Hayek suggests governments should anticipate such institutions, and encourage their inter-competitive growth so that the strongest and most effective institutions emerge spontaneously and keep each other on their toes through unceasing competition.

The limits of bureaucracies

One trap that most democratic and other countries have fallen into, however, is precisely that of infallibilist illusions. For instance, it is possible for an individual to defraud another set of individuals by claiming to have a company with prospects for significant business, and solicit investments based on false information. This has clearly happened in every society from the beginning of civilization. But the modern response has been to set up a government-sponsored bureaucracy staffed with people who are to certify each solicitation of investment. But the staff is as subject to fallibility of knowledge as any individual or group. The bureaucracy therefore only succeeds in falsely lulling the public into thinking that government-certified solicitations of investment are safe, whereas in fact the government agency cannot have the power to guarantee that, given the inescapable fact of fallibility. In this case, the government could, for instance, simply mandate certain minimum information disclosure requirements, and allow the spontaneous development of private rating agencies that will examine that information and provide the public third-party ratings on the apparent reliability and potential of the investment. Indeed, the more trustworthy private rating agencies may end up refusing to certify a solicitation unless a larger amount of information is disclosed than the minimum disclosure mandated by government. Once new effective disclosure requirements are discovered by the competitive rating agencies, the government can also update the mandated disclosure requirements, allowing the system to be self-maintaining and preventing obsolescence of regulations.

Such disclosure requirements are one form of the use of coercive government power, but coercion of a lesser degree than the fraud it tries to guard against. Punishment in most democratic countries is also similarly and wisely restricted to a form of coercion less than the coercion outlawed, which would tend to build confidence of the public in the government that it is true to the principle of a minimized level of coercion in society. Indeed, it is hard to defend capital punishment, an act of irreversible coercion, in the face of provable fallibility of knowledge, since it implies that convictions may be arrived at in error. It is impossible to justify any act of coercion because all justifications are provably fallible, so the least one can do is to use the presumption of innocence and require a legal due process that maintains some basic rights of the accused.

The negative nature of good law

Hayek spent a large amount of time writing about the nature of laws that are appropriate for a government to make, given the fact that the lawmakers themselves are fallible. He was also an avid reader of the work of Lord Acton, whose most famous quotation is that 'power tends to corrupt, and absolute power corrupts absolutely'. If we restrict the legislative branch of democratic government to only make laws that are negative, i.e., that ban or outlaw specific action rather than try to exhaustively list the allowable actions, and have these laws interpreted by an independent judiciary, then we do not run the risk of the laws restricting competitive discovery of new knowledge. For instance, when a new phenomenon such as the Internet emerges, instead of specifying what the allowable actions on the Internet are, the law need only concern itself with outlawing any form of coercion that occurs on the Internet, such as misrepresentation and fraud. Indeed, with a constitution protecting individual rights, such coercion would already be illegal despite no specific written law about it. Making new laws only serves to formalize the outlaw of and remedies to specific forms of coercion that emerge under new and changing circumstances. Hayek calls this a process of private or non-formal law, which emerges first from free human action, and public or written law only being the formalization of this discovered rule. But in addition to observing human peacetime interaction (which usually spontaneously demands minimized coercion) to discover new law, the *principle* of non-coercion can effectively be used to determine which actions should be formally outlawed. There is no cause to suggest that once we have outlawed coercion then no more law is required. Rather, every time a society makes progress to clearly define a type of coercion, a new law can be made outlawing that specific type of coercion and providing for appropriate remedies. For instance, even though violence is clearly illegal, there is no harm in passing more laws to highlight specific forms of violence targeted at specific groups, and specifically outlawing it and specifying a particular punishment for those found guilty. Such 'hate crime' legislation has typically found its way into most democratic governments, though out of just plain common sense rather than high theory. The idea that hate crime legislation is superfluous and therefore not needed seems nonsensical, given the fact that fallibility forces us to be as precise and complete as we can.

Corruption

The one thing to avoid at virtually all costs is making laws that give government bureaucrats discretionary power. Here, Lord Acton's caution comes into magnificent display. Every time in history that governments create positions of discretionary power, what happens is that sooner or later the worst of people—the people with no compunctions about coercing others—will claw their way into being appointed to that post. Once they are there, they will use and abuse that discretionary power to their own advantage—whether they use it for financial advantage or other advantages such as ideological, political, or social varies from society to society and individual to individual. It is useless for countries to give discretionary power to bureaucrats and then expect that there would be no corruption. As Hayek points out, the only solution is to ensure that the laws that are passed by a democratic government are required to be general, abstract, universally applicable, equally applicable to all citizens including government servants, negative rather than prescriptive in nature, and contain no grant of discretionary power to a bureaucracy. This does not mean that laws should be completely unambiguous—in fact, the incompleteness theorem and the nature of language guarantees that situations will arise where the law seems ambiguous. But in this case, it is the duty of the judicial system to interpret the law from the standpoint of a ban on coercive actions, and based on presentations of all the facts by all the concerned parties. Bureaucracies, if needed at all in government, need only serve various procedural and secretarial aspects of government. Decision-making need not and should not be part of the bureaucratic task. In fact, with the advent of inexpensive information technology and networks, all tasks of government can potentially be automated once bureaucratic decision-making is removed.

Property rights

It is a small step of deduction to go from the premise of a ban on coercion, to an implication of property rights. For instance, if you had possession of some object, I would be unable to take it away from you without coercion or your consent. This automatically implies a right to property. Now, there has been copious literature in the West over the last 350 years to show the benefits of laws explicitly protecting property rights. What Hayek shows us, however, is that this right is not "immanent" or somehow transcendentally existent. It is simply a logical consequence of a ban on coercion, which itself is a logical consequence of the axiom of fallibility. Property rights also allow those individuals interested in increasing their properties to competitively provide goods and services, continually driving the prices of such goods and services down due to such competition.

The reduced prices, or in other words, improved productivity, allow increases in the general standard of living in the society and constant striving for new knowledge to produce new forms of productivity growth and wealth. A non-competitive centrally planned economic system would not spontaneously generate a demand for new knowledge and technology. In fact, given the technical excellence of scientists in "second" and "third" world countries such as Russia and India, it is fairly safe to assume that the technological superiority of the West is more because there is a demand for technology due to competitive pressures, rather than a superior supply of technology. As I will discuss in the chapter on entrepreneurship, it seems that demand needs to precede supply.

The group that most vehemently opposed property rights was, of course, the Marxists. Hayek spent much of his time showing that the central planning alternative to a property rights based system would fail precisely because of the inherent fallibility of knowledge. But in an age where science was held to be a source of infallible knowledge, Marxist movements all over the world tried to implement the ideas. It should be mentioned however, that the Marxist movement itself came from a time when the idea of property rights was held in esteem, but the concept that coercion should be banned was not particularly popular or known. Indeed if we assume individual liberty is not restricted by a morality to refrain from coercion, then we would take liberty as a license to coerce, as long as such coercion were not explicitly encoded as illegal in explicitly written law. In Marx's time, many industrialists and wealth owners routinely indulged in coercive use of their discretionary power—some of them in fairly extreme acts of coercion. It is not surprising then that many poorer people effectively thought that all accumulation of wealth must have involved some coercion. Today, in economically advanced democracies, overt coercion is not indulged in on a broad scale and most wealth creation is from superior knowledge and technology and talent, but many forms of coercion still persist and are popularly considered legitimate under the umbrella of individual and economic liberty.

Fortunately, history has shown that socialist central planning cannot succeed and Hayek's concepts have clearly prevailed. But the issue now needs to revert to the original question that Hayek explains as the philosophy of the Old Whigs, a 17th century group of philosophers that preceded the major Enlightenment philosophers of the 18th century such as Adam Smith and David Hume. The Old Whigs came from a religious background, where fallibility was taken for granted, and where liberty clearly implied as much the liberty of others as oneself, implying that coercion was ruled out. The current post-socialism issue then becomes to democratically debate what expressions of our individual freedom might not be legitimate and might in fact coerce others. This issue may have got tempered and lost to some degree in years following the Old Whigs as the belief in infallible science and unrestrained economic and individual liberty grew, but it is an idea that must resurface, now that socialism has been dispensed with. Some contemporary questions include:

- If I have you sign a contract with me but do not disclose pertinent information that I have, is this not coercion?

- If I sell you a product I know to be defective and do not tell you, is this not coercion?

- If I sell you a product that I know is harmful but neglect to tell you, is it not coercion?

- If I have a monopoly in some industry necessary for your survival and I refuse to sell to you unless you buy another of my products or refrain from buying some other product, is this not coercion?

Monopolies

The last question in the preceding paragraph brings up an issue that needs to be addressed. If knowledge discovery occurs primarily through a competitive process, then it should follow that a monopoly provider would not be able to rapidly increase knowledge (and thereby improve productivity and profit) precisely because of a lack of competition. So it seems that unless the monopoly is in a field that is very old and there is no substantial new knowledge to be gained, it is not in a company's interest to acquire all of its competitors solely to make profit-making easier. Free market theorists have argued that monopolies are not necessarily bad, because it is in the monopolies interest to provide various pricing schemes to reach all of the additional customers that it can reach. However, this is only true of a monopoly owner who is a completely rational being. In practice, however, fallible human beings with prejudices and peculiarities of their own would be in charge of decisions. It would be in the power of the monopolist to coercively use discretionary power, and those coerced may not be in a position of sufficient power to seek redress.

Hayek while pointing out that monopoly itself is not necessarily bad, the power to coerce is potentially troubling. He provides an example of the owner of the only oasis in a desert community. Now, in normal, competitive scenarios, business owners may choose who they do business with and who they choose not to do business with. Hayek admits that this is precisely the way that the oasis owner might abuse his discretionary power. For instance he may choose to make people follow a particular religion or belief, or else refuse to sell water. But instead of advocating a necessity to split up the monopoly into competing entities, Hayek suggests that we could remove the power to discretionary sell to some people and not others. The oasis owner would have to publish a price list at which he would sell various quantities of water at various times, but any individual in the society would be free to purchase the water on those terms. The term "free water" in this desert society would refer to the freedom of access rather than suggesting that water be provided free-of-charge, the latter of which would lead only to over-use and depletion of resources.

The same situation might rise today in any number of fields from commodity supply businesses to high technology businesses. While it may not be necessary to break up any companies (though one would assume that they themselves might voluntarily want to retain some competition in order to hasten the knowledge discovery process and increase productivity) it may sometimes be necessary to mandate that they provide free access at a published price list and cannot refuse to deal with certain customers on a discretionary basis.

In high technology areas involving interacting technologies provided by market participants, a dominant player might use coercion by simply not publishing interface standards. The role of the law then could simply be to mandate disclosure of interfaces by publishing the underlying software code universally, and providing access to hardware interfaces at a particular price list.

Artificial monopolies: intellectual property

Given the set of deductions that we have used thus far, it is not surprising to find that while Hayek recommended full protection of property rights for physical property, he felt that this does not automatically suggest the same protection for intellectual property. This is because it is not clear how one user of intellectual property is coerced if another user also uses the same property—something that is impossible for physical property. In fact, the intellectual property owner is the one who has the power to coerce by agreeing to deal with some customers and refusing to deal with others.

A practical solution would be to extend Hayek's description of limiting the discretionary power of monopoly holders by forcing them to state a price list at which they would license their property to anyone who wants to use it. Since intellectual property once created requires no manufacturing costs, a step further might be to require the property right holder to provide the price as a percentage of value-added so that the intellectual property can be used in economies that will only sustain lower prices, and so that competitive producers of goods that use the intellectual property will drive prices lower and productivity higher.

Freedom of knowledge does not mean that knowledge must be given free-of-charge, only the freedom to spread. In fact, once knowledge is given freedom to disperse spontaneously, it may in fact provide the property right holder more sales and income than if restricted to discretionary distribution. For instance, a patent holder would state a price or percentage of value added for licensing the patented product, rather than require elaborate negotiations in which the patent owner exercises discretionary coercive power. If we believe that coercion is economically inefficient, we could expect that the total profit to the patent holder derived from such "frictionless commerce" would be higher than the profit derived by pretending to infallibly know the optimum way of licensing the patent. In the area of copyrights too, while publishing companies play a significant role in publicity and promotion and general stimulation of demand, it could be conceivable that the creative writer or artist and a promotions company declare a joint copyright and royalty sharing agreement, and then let any number of publishing companies manufacture and distribute copies as long as they pay a standard royalty amount or percentage of added value.

Market failure

Although we show that free competition tends to lower costs and increase productivity and quality, there can be situations where competition on price alone can cause commonly owned assets—such as the air we breathe, for instance—to become lower in quality. That is, markets can fail to remove coercion spontaneously, and government action may be needed. For example, cars may pollute and cause the property value of all local citizens to drop, which is a form of coercion against their property rights. Now, if one car company makes cleaner cars, they may be out-competed by other car companies. Now what has historically happened is the democratic protest has forced the government to act, and they have created bureaucracies to mandate certain types of pollution controlling technologies. But because knowledge is fallible, we have no idea whether the mandated technology is the cheapest or most productive way to reduce pollution. Here the government has fallen into the trap of infallibilist illusion and brought a screeching halt to the process of competitive knowledge discovery. This is not to say that there was not a market failure in the first place, but the government needs to react by creating structures that allow innovation to reduce costs over time. For instance, if the government created a fund where the current level of pollution was measured and, say, one billion shares (the number is irrelevant) were issued as the rights to pollute to that level. Then companies are forced to buy the amount of rights to pollute that their cars (or other machines) need, and pass that cost on to their customers. This creates an incentive to discover more efficient technologies that will accomplish the end result—the reduction of that type of pollution—even without the government knowing beforehand exactly how the competitive players will eventually achieve that result. The government can then set a target of reduction in emissions by some percentage each year so that the competitive players would be incented to continually improve technologies and reduce pollution.

Under this type of regulation where markets are artificially created by democratic government to re-engineer incentives, it really does not matter whether the fear that society democratically agrees to be fearful of is a fully justified fear or not. For instance, there is scientific debate over whether global warming is really caused by greenhouse gas emissions from man-made machines or whether apparent global warming and cooling are macro-geological effects that are not affected much by man-made emissions. But if we have sufficient cause to believe that man-made greenhouse gases should be reduced just in case, and if we can democratically agree to it, then we can set up a right-to-emit fund for greenhouse gases, starting from whatever present level it is at and progressively improve things over time. Using such self-organizing or "spontaneously ordered" systems, there will be no significant artificial barrier placed on the core knowledge discovery process of competitive markets that is at the root of productivity improvement and wealth creation.

POVERTY

There is no doubt that poverty is undesirable, and disturbing to anyone who has ordinary human emotions. But another source of bungling by governments has come out of the desire to legislate a ban on poverty. But as Hayek points out, it is no use legislating a wish or desire and passing that as a directive to a bureaucracy. That bureaucrat cannot possibly possess the knowledge or ability to accomplish that goal—either we have to be more specific in what the bureaucrat should do, or just not legislate an undefined wish. But on the other hand, free market fundamentalists have held that if only governments did nothing at all, they are infallibly sure that there would be no poverty. Since this is clearly not historically evidenced, as well as unlikely in the face of evidence that market failures can occur, many people reject this completely. Given fallibility and the desirability for a society free of coercion of individuals by other individuals, it is unsurprising that Hayek found such *laissez-faire* theory to be sterile.

The truth seems to be that there are systemic structural issues that keep certain types of people and families constantly disadvantaged and poor. Such a condition of persistent coercion is called oppression, but the coercion we are talking about here is not necessarily something where any individual is deliberately coercing the people who are stuck in a poverty trap. Rather, this is a situation where the condition of oppressive poverty has occurred spontaneously. But there is no cause to blame a wealthy person or set of wealthy persons for this state of spontaneous coercion, as Marx and his followers attempted to do. Though there may be many wealthy people who coerce other individuals less powerful than them-selves, it is the coercion and not the wealth that should be banned, while techniques to help the powerless individual acquire wealth need to be dis-covered. We therefore first need to look at the way that we have been able to define coercion, especially in the Hayekian sense of defining fraud as coercion and non-disclosure of certain types of information as coercion.

Once we define non-disclosure to be coercive, it is easily conceivable that many people, if not all people, are guilty of at least small acts of coer-cion. Of course, it is not practical or advisable for the state to involve itself in every such act of disclosure-related coercion. Non-disclosure is consid-ered coercion in most democracies only if it constituted material fraud—most democratic governments will only enforce contracts if all pertinent information has been disclosed. But it is the function of democratic debate and scientific inquiry to study the conditions leading to sponta-neous oppression and poverty. Particularly, to see whether certain disclo-sure requirements might be legislated to create pathways for those people stuck in oppressive poverty to help themselves out of it.

In the following chapters we discuss the following specific forms of coercion:

- Non-disclosure in banking
- Non-disclosure in education
- Non-disclosure of knowledge of what makes entrepreneurship and wealth creation successful.

In each of these situations, there is a spontaneous incentive for the peo-ple who are aware of this non-disclosure to keep the undisclosed informa-tion private. In other words there would be a demand for this information were it available, but there is a market failure to supply this demand. The outcome of this market failure is systemic and enduring poverty for some groups of people, and the chapters that follow show how this market fail-ure can be overcome and systemic poverty virtually eliminated.

Hayek also points out that there is also no substantial prevention of the competitive knowledge discovery process if governments create schemes for subsistence welfare. Even 17th and 18th century Britain—the first country to undergo the huge changes in the relative value of knowledge that accompanies industrial growth—had what was known as the Poor Law, which provided for basic subsistence initially for the landless laborers no longer needed due to rises in agricultural productivity. Indeed, even if systemic poverty is eliminated, fallibility ensures that from time to time, those who are successful may suffer sudden misfortune and lose all their wealth, and perhaps some abilities. In such cases, the government could provide for a minimum subsistence if the electorate so wished, without causing any destruction of the underlying knowledge discovery and wealth creation process. Hayek cautions that though the government may give financial assistance through some kind of negative income tax that established a minimum income level, but they should not seek to create monopolistic bureaucracies to deliver it. They should instead allow competitive private players to deliver the basic services to the recipients of basic welfare and let the welfare recipients choose the providers they want. This could be done, for instance, by issuing food stamps, clothing stamps, shelter stamps, and healthcare stamps that could be used to purchase food, clothing, shelter, and heath insurance from competitive private players. A monopolistic bureaucracy that provides the services rather than the targeted subsidy is sure to distort the knowledge discovery process by crowding out the competitive process. Hayek also agreed that in wealthy countries the level of welfare might also be deemed to be higher than a level of basic physical subsistence.

To take the concept of basic welfare further, it is also conceivable that basic financial assistance to the indigent can be structured as an at-risk loan. Those that work themselves back to a degree of self-sustenance can repay their loans as a percentage of their earnings until it is fully paid back, but those who do not manage to do so would not pay it back as long as their income remained below what was defined as subsistence in that nation. Once we study the nature of banking and bank credit, it will become clear how any country, including poor or developing countries, might use this technique, which we will discuss again in the chapter on Development Economics.

Money & Banking

The history of money

Money is a very poorly understood entity and is best understood by studying how it emerged historically. In the early days of societies all over the world, people used barter to exchange goods that one had and another wanted. It most societies, however, this leads to a system where some artifact—whether it is gold or silver or copper or beads or shells—is used to represent the relative value of goods, and transactions can be carried out using money rather than barter. This leads to a direct incentive for people to circumvent having to produce something others need by simply searching for the article that represents money—for example, gold. It follows that most societies that succeeded in producing an economy where people spent more time producing what people need rather than simply looking for some artifact were societies that chose naturally rare objects or metals to represent money. In most major societies including ancient Egypt, India, China, Greece, and Rome, gold became the object that was used to represent money. Most also had economies where silver and copper and other metals were also used as subsidiary or alternate currencies. When a metal-based currency is used, money serves both as a store of value—an investment or savings in the asset—as well as a unit of account, i.e. a scale upon which we price all commercially available things.

Credit and bank notes

The next step for an economy is to move from a money-based economy further to a credit based economy. Initially, societies start by a lender of money actually lending coins to a borrower. But around 1200 AD, a banking system resembling the modern one emerged, first in Venice, and then in all Europe. In a banking regime, a banker's word or note serves as a representation of his promise to pay up the equivalent gold or other specified asset. In such a regime, notes soon become more commonly used than hard currency. With the development of telegraphic technology, it also became possible for banks to have branches in multiple cities and countries to facilitate payments between inter-city and international traders. Banks also became the caretakers of the underlying gold represented by the notes they issued. Banks would therefore only deal with banks that were trusted and if notes were issued by a lesser known bank or a bank owned by people of lesser wealth, then those notes would only be accepted at a discount off the face value. This sort of free-wheeling banking reached its height in the newly colonized territories of America, where so-called "wildcat" banking referred to banks in places where only wildcats would go.

It is important to note that when banks gave loans to entrepreneurs, they always took some form of collateral. For this reason, most loans were only given to entrepreneurial ventures sponsored by people who were already wealthy or propertied. If the venture failed and the loan could not be repaid, the asset would be confiscated by the bank. Since notes were being used in place of gold or metal, the act of making a loan to an enterprise became a simple matter of making an entry in the banks books that this collateral was now pledged to the bank, and in turn the bank creates a deposit—a number of pounds or lire or dollars that is put in an account that the bank deems is owned by the enterprise taking the loan. Once this system takes hold it becomes clear to the banking community that it is really not necessary to maintain a stock of gold equal to the value of the currency in circulation. After all, there was collateral backing up the creation of that deposit. The only reason to maintain some level of gold reserves was because from time to time the borrower would need to make payments in cash, and therefore require a withdrawal of gold. But it was clear by this point that there was no need to hold an amount of gold equal to the amount of new money created by the stroke of a pen as a loan or deposit for the borrower.

This is an astounding and amazing development in history then. Basically, it had become possible for banks to essentially become manufacturers of money. But bank credit is not permanent money—it must be returned as per an agreed schedule, with interest. It is a temporary creation of money, but if used to generate a profit, the profit remains as permanent money—true wealth—even after the loan has been repaid. How much of such credit-money the banks manufactured depended on how much collateral the borrowers were willing to put up, or whatever risks the banker was willing to take if collateral was insufficient. The automatic check on the banker taking too much risk is that other bankers need to have confidence in him. If other banks start refusing to accept notes underwritten by a particular bank, then that bank's whole business model is in trouble. Clearly, if a bank over-stretches and creates too many notes, or accepts dubious collateral, or finances risky ventures, then there will be a reduction in the value at which other banks accept the note. To keep a check on this, movement of gold from bank to bank became the way that credit creation was automatically limited. By maintaining a convention of how much in gold reserves banks had to keep to satisfy other banks enough to accept their notes, there was a systemic limitation on the amount of lending or money creation that a bank could undertake.

It is also important to note that employees of an enterprise would also be often paid in the notes of the bank that issued a loan to the enterprise. Employees would also maintain bank accounts in that bank, so when credit is created as an entry in the bank ledgers, when it moves to the employees account, it is simply a transfer of data from one ledger to another. Information was essentially becoming the entity used to represent money, though at this point it was still convertible to gold. As banks became reputable, it became possible for banks to collect more deposits than they themselves created by offering interest on deposits from the public. These deposits appear as liabilities on a bank balance sheet, and the loans appear as assets. As long as the assets yield a return higher than the cost of interest on the liabilities, a bank remains profitable. The actual cash needed as capital to be eligible to conduct this business of manufacturing money was represented by the gold reserve requirement.

Central banking: going off gold

In the twentieth century the world went off the gold standard for reasons beyond the scope of this book. But it was replaced by a government sponsored system of having a central monetary authority that specified the proportion of assets that a bank should maintain in reputable assets, namely debt to the government treasury or Treasury Bonds as they are known, or other hard assets such as land and equity capital contributed by the owners of the bank and maintained as cash. Further, international institutions such as the Basle Committee maintain guidelines that banks across countries should maintain if they want to build the confidence that facilitates payments across borders. The modern system then becomes basically one that mimics the gold reserve system, without actually needing gold convertibility.

The problem that arose was that once it also became tempting for the government to try and coerce the monetary authority to relax reserve standards and increase the amount of lending in the economy in an attempt to speed up economic growth. But what emerged is that if we create more money than the economy is able to absorb in new projects that produce goods that others actually want, then what happens is that the economy adjusts by increasing the prices of goods generally to absorb the available money, i.e. it causes inflation. Internationally, the consequence was that countries that were lax on their reserve requirements and created too much money ended up taking a hit by a decline in the value of their currency. In fact, the Bretton Woods Institutions of the IMF and the World Bank were set up to try to prevent this from happening, but essentially the free float of currencies against each other became impossible to prevent as long as governments arbitrarily used their monopoly on coercive power to interfere with lending standards. Currency trading was the only way for the financial markets to keep some sanity to the meaning of money as representative of what people hold valuable.

The inherent instability of credit

But it is not as if the above system of banking and credit creation was flawless before governments became controllers of reserve asset requirements. A deeper instability has always pervaded the Western model of banking and bank credit creation, though credit creation has been the prime driver of growth in the Western economies as well as growth in science and technology (since economic competition produces greater and greater need for new knowledge that increases the profits, to offset decreasing margins caused by competition). The inherent instability of credit stems from a mismatch in the liquidity demand of the holders of liabilities (deposits) in banks and the liquidity available on the assets (loans) created by the banks. In times of crisis or uncertainty, holders of deposits want to increase their liquid holdings and may demand more cash or cash equivalents such as Treasury Bonds. Banks may be forced to call in loans to balance out assets and liabilities, creating a general business downturn. In such a situation the bank may be unable to raise liquid assets and cash in sufficient quantity to meet liquidity demands even though it calls in loans and shuts down companies and repossess collateral, because there is a general preference for liquidity in the whole economy due to the uncertainty. At this point banks may shut down and depositors may lose their deposits.

Non-disclosure as coercion

If we look at the situation from a point of view of coercion and disclosure, we can clearly see that the depositors in a bank need to know that such a liquidity mismatch situation can occur, especially during times of great fear or uncertainty. We must note at this point that money is not really an asset in itself but only as good as the set of loans on the other side of the bank's balance sheet. People upset about this non-disclosure have included various fringe groups advocating that banks should not make loans at all and keep depositors money as cash. Of course, then there would not be any credit creation at all, certainly no interest payments on deposits, and probably no economic activity at all and no jobs to give depositors any money to deposit in the first place.

In the extreme case, the downturn never reverses because the money creation engine has been shut down, resulting in a persistent economic depression where no one takes risks, no one is willing to finance risks, and as a result no one earns any profits—a vicious cycle that perpetuates itself. There have been many academic suggestions for correcting this situation, most notably by J.M. Keynes, and there is still debate on whether corrections taken on the basis of Keynesian theory were appropriate or not. At any rate they were corrections suggested by a theory, which in turn is necessarily fallible, so it is almost sure that the theory was not the best possible way to remedy the situation or to prevent it occurring in the first place. Milton Friedman is known for a modification of Keynes theories that teach us how to prevent inflation created by too much creation of money via bank credit. Friedman's quantity theory of money has become the accepted practice for countries around the world that now tend to leave their monetary authorities alone to manage the quantity of credit money allowed in the economy. But it is still not clear whether Friedman's recommendation of watching the price levels of certain goods to determine whether to allow more credit or less credit to be created is necessarily effective. After all, there can never be complete knowledge accumulated in one central place such as a monetary authority—there is simply too much knowledge in the economy for this to be possible. Another problem is that there is no reason why price levels should be stable—in fact, with constant productivity increases due to competition, we should expect continually declining prices of older types of goods where there are more competitors, while newer types of goods would be able to sustain higher prices for a while. Indeed monetary authorities today are sometimes quite foxed about whether to increase bank credit or reduce it or what unintended effect their actions may have. We have periods of tremendous growth with no inflation and periods of inflation without any growth in the economy, which seems to suggest there is more to things than Friedman explains.

Hayek also had some theories about business cycles and monetary policy that do not require an omniscient central monetary authority, much of which has not been taken seriously after he effectively, in the pubic eye, lost the debate to Keynes. More recent developments in financial markets however, point to an interesting fundamental change in the banking system that, while being not exactly what Hayek suggested, has very similar properties. This development is known as securitization.

Securitization: the disintermediation of deposits

It is a banker's constant dream to be able to create as much credit as he can get away with creating. It is only the credit and compliance department of banks that restrains them. After all a lender is not a buyer—he is a seller, a seller who is selling money for a profit. In the 1970's, as countries were restricting their banks' extent of lending using government regulation, market players found ways to create credit that got around lending limits. Banks realized that they could make loans and sell the loans off to people with money to invest. These loans then go off the balance sheet, and then more loans can be made without breaking the reserve requirements. It is important to note that when markets find ways around rules that essentially serve to prevent coercion, it is not necessary that their work around is coercive in any way. Indeed, there is no one the worse when a set of loans gets sold off the bank's balance sheet. The person who bought them would otherwise have had to put their money in a savings deposit and then have a bank make loans using that deposit base, and the bank would take the profit margin. In this new mode, the investor or saver invests directly in bonds that are basically a package of loans. The risk is taken by this investor, as are the profits. In practice, the world of securitization—the packaging of sets of loans into bonds and selling them off balance sheet—expanded in the US initially only in loans made on residential property where the loans were counter-guaranteed by government-sponsored institutions. But since then, it has expanded to almost every conceivable type of loan or other financial asset.

The second level of complexity comes when banks, realizing that this is a win-win deal for all concerned, start trying to increase the level of securitization. The first step is to use a tool called credit enhancement. In this, the bank selling the securitized pool of loans essentially tells the buyer that they will assume the first, say, 8% of losses on the loans. Now since there is a pool of several loans, and since the seller is offering to take the first 8% of losses *no matter which loan defaults*, the loans in the pool insure each other and the seller is providing additional insurance so the buyer of this "credit-enhanced" bond has less risk. So in this case, the seller of securitized bonds has basically taken out some of the risk on the pool of loans in order to be able to sell it off the balance sheet. In effect, two tranches have been created out of a pool—92% of the pool is in the "senior" tranche that takes the last losses and 8% is in a "subordinate" tranche that takes the first losses up to a maximum of 8% of the pool.

The next level of complexity that emerged is to create, instead of a two-tier senior-subordinate structure, a bank can create what is know as a "waterfall"—a multi-tiered structure of senior, mezzanine, and subordinate tranches. The waterfall is defined by the percentage of the pool that is assigned to each tranche. Payments on the loans are routed first to the senior-most tranche and then flow down the waterfall. Conversely, losses are borne first by the most subordinate tranche and then flow upward. Further innovation has allowed banks to separate different types of risk—for example, principal default risk from interest rate risk. Other innovations include liquidity options to buy or sell the bonds at some point in the future, and currency risk options. Every aspect of risk can be named and separated out using a waterfall structure, and the risk can be held by those investors that are comfortable about that type of risk. So we see that though fallibility is not academically discussed, the financial market is well aware of fallibility and continues to innovate to hedge against various defaults on our fallible expectations. It is important to note that risk is not eliminated—it is only managed by explicitly splitting out various types of risk, using insurance strategies, and selling each type of risk to those who explicitly want to hold that risk in exchange for potential profit. A pension fund that seeks very safe investments can invest only in secure senior tranches of securitization deals. A hedge fund that manages the speculative capital of wealthy people and institutions may want to buy a whole portfolio of riskier subordinate tranches, in the anticipation that even if some of them perform and some do not, their return will be higher than in a safe senior note.

Looking back at our 20th century model of banks as institutions that take deposits on the one hand and make loans on the other, we see that the reality of modern finance has changed the picture quite fundamentally. The bond market in general (including securitized bonds as well as bonds issued directly by individual companies and institutions) has allowed investors to place money directly as loans, bypassing the deposit-centric banking system. We earlier discussed that the implicit coercion in a deposit-centric banking system was that there is not really full disclosure to the depositor that there is a serious risk of mismatch in liquidity— although the depositor thinks he has funds available in cash, it actually depends on the banks ability to liquidate loans of a longer maturity, which is sometimes impossible in a major market downturn. If this risk is properly disclosed, it is almost certain that depositors would ask their banks what insurance they had against this. In this case, there would be a huge surge in demand for safe bonds to store money in but clearly a small retail saver has no ability to decide whether to put money in bonds of Company A or Company B. The world of securitization provides the precise tools that banks can use to take whatever loan supply, or in other words "risk supply" there is in the market, and transform it using securitization to a set of tranches with a different risk profile that is dependent on the design of the waterfall structure. Securitization becomes a tool to re-engineer the risk supply in any economy and to tailor it exactly to the demand for risk in that economy. In the extreme case, "cash" becomes a fiction. Each person would hold their money in securities of their choice, and bear the risk of the market value of that security rising or falling. In this case, the liquidity mismatch of deposit-centric banking that causes banking system crashes becomes impossible. There is no cause for a small saver to fear this regime since it is fairly easy for a bank to use securitization and options to create a security that is very safe, as long as the investor is willing to accept an interest rate that is probably lower than the average rate of return on capital in the economy.

Hayek: toward a Quality Theory of money

Although Hayek did not and could not have anticipated the securitized bond market, he did outline a theory of capital and a monetary policy that essentially allowed any number of privately owned currencies to be used as legal tender in an economy, rather than one national currency. The purpose of this was so that the owner of the currency would take the role of finding ways to monitor credit risk of loans provided in that currency, and then competitive discovery would eventually yield the most optimal ways of managing credit risk. Now converting all credit into bonds and securitized products is analogous to competitive currencies because each type of bond would trade in the bond market, and if people felt that, for instance, bonds to technology companies were becoming risky they would sell those bonds and the price of those bonds would fall, just like a currency that the market does not like would fall if the quality of credit was not trusted. This would indicate to the people making loans in the first place not to increase lending in the technology sector because the myriad players in the market each of whom hold some particular knowledge have collectively decided that money supply (i.e. credit supply) to that portion of the economy needs to slow down. But this does not necessarily affect the price of, say, a senior tranche of securitized residential mortgages, and the price of those bonds might actually rise at the same time that the price of technology bonds are falling. So the economy does not suffer a general fall in credit supply, but simply moves money supply around from one area to another, from one date of maturity to another, and from one risk level to another. Moving to less risky instruments would automatically mean taking less profits (or "yield" as net interest income on a bond is called), which increases the incentive from people with extra wealth and risk taking ability to step in and buy bonds that become perceived as too risky for small, safety-oriented investors. Thus money supply is not being regulated as some collectivized entity by a central monetary authority. Money supply can expand in one area and contract in another area at the same time, and no central authority with complete knowledge is needed. For instance, lending can increase in home buying and student loans, while simultaneously decreasing in convertible bonds from loss-making companies and margin debt accounts for purchasing stock.

Another point to note is that the bond market and the securitization market in particular demands a very high level of disclosure of data. No one would buy a bond if historical data on the bond performance or its underlying assets were not fully disclosed. Disclosure—in other words reduced coercion—is in this case being mandated spontaneously by market forces. If securitization and the use of public bond markets rather than deposit-centric banks becomes universal, there is no need for the central monetary authority to control quantity of bank credit because if a bank created new credit it would need to sell it to specific bond holders, who would not buy it unless they were willing to hold that particular risk. The market can regulate quality of bank credit spontaneously as long as this principle of full disclosure is maintained. The quantity of bank credit becomes irrelevant as long as the quality of credit is good, and there is no fixed theoretical limit on the amount of money supply growth or economic growth that is possible without general unproductive inflation in prices of all goods. Any number of private banks could participate in this money creation process, though they would be limited by the markets willingness to buy the specific assets.

A synthetic unit of account

The currency's role as a unit of account—a common unit used to express prices in—could continue, but if a currency mandated all debt created in that currency to be publicly traded, that currency would essentially be a stable and predictable one since only the specific bad debts that prove to be bad will lose value and not the currency itself. The currency itself simply becomes a synthetic number derivable from the price of all the bonds in the economy. Investors would deposit their money in bonds rather than collectivized 'deposits' that pretend to be risk-free, and when making payments, they would liquidate a bond at the rate it is quoted in the synthetic currency and the recipient of the money would simultaneously choose which bonds to place the money in on receipt. Such a synthetic currency is therefore basically a currency that is used only for pricing and it would be nonsensical to hold the currency as a store of value outside of holding any specific sets of bonds that are quoted in that currency. Currency trading in its current sense would not be possible since one would have to decide which particular bonds denominated in that currency one wanted to buy or sell and not just buy or sell the currency itself. Of course, cross-currency risk derivatives—futures and options—could still be created, bought, and sold. Such a system would in effect provide all the benefits that Hayek's proposal of competitive currencies could offer, and more, since there can now be a globally used unit of account, while the stores of value—i.e. bonds—are forced to be competitive.

ENTREPRENEURSHIP

The nature of demand

In classical economics texts, an entrepreneur is basically an agent who is quick to spot demand for goods and services and changes in that demand, and arranges for the production of those goods. A variation on that theme, known as Say's Law, contends that "supply creates its own demand"—i.e., (1) that the customer needs to see what is available before developing a desire for it, and (2) that a part of the capital budget of an entrepreneurial venture includes creation of the demand for the goods being produced. In light of fallibility, of course, we would need to modify Say's Law to state that supply might (or might not) succeed in creating its own demand. What we intend to achieve in this chapter is to prove that demand creation must precede supply, and a more useful law is that demand creates its own supply.

In the face of extremely competitive modern markets, there has been a general reversal of the importance of production versus demand creation. Demand creation in the form of branding, marketing and sales has come to be recognized as the primary entrepreneurial task. Even technology, which is obviously useful to reduce costs and improve productivity, has a larger role to play in demand creation by creating a perceived need to be using the latest technology in order to remain competitive in the future. Of course there is always a business opportunity in taking a market in which demand already exists, and using technology and innovation to capture some of that demand by lowering the price, improving the quality, etc. But that is more of an arbitrage opportunity than creation of original demand. Such arbitrage opportunities are an important part of an economy, but if we were to restrict ourselves to producing only those things for which there is already demand, then Marx's prediction that capitalism would compete itself out of profit would indeed be true. Marx's logic clearly applies in that competition has the net effect of reducing profits, yet we find evidence that the aggregate level of profit in modern competitive economies has not started to approach zero. The reason for this is that entrepreneurs are creating demand for things not previously existent.

The true entrepreneur who is not reducible to a Marxian caricature therefore is an agent that creates demand for things that currently have no proven market, or branded items that by definition have no competition. Given a free society, there is no way that one person can force another person to desire or need something. But given human nature, all individuals are born by default with desire. Human desire may be for material things beginning with food, shelter, and clothing; or non-material needs such as self-discovery, love, attention, peace of mind, etc. J. K. Galbraith tried to make the point that creation of desire by entrepreneurs using advertising and marketing strategies was somehow not moral or at least something that is not to be assigned the exalted status that writers such as Adam Smith confer upon entrepreneurs. But Hayek responded by pointing out that in a free society, once we get beyond basic subsistence needs of food, shelter, and clothing, practically all our "needs" are cultural in nature. It is an artifact of culture that makes people feel they need, say, a hat of a certain style, or a religious statue or object of some kind, basically because not having it while their friends and neighbors have it causes their peace of mind to be disturbed.

A general theory of culture

Now let us snap back to philosophy for a bit, and discuss the nature of our selves and our desires as human individuals. In a world in which we realize that all knowledge is fallible, the one type of knowledge that is not fallible is cultural artifact. If in a group of people a set of people thinks that a certain type of music or a certain style of clothing is attractive, then they do. There is no right or wrong about it, though typically styles only succeed in attracting people if they have reflected some theme of nature—such as standard beats in music expressing the nature of time in the material world, or a style of clothing that reflects the nature of water falling, etc. All of these things help to reinforce the Ramanuja conjecture of the material world as existent despite any infallible knowledge about it through our minds. The need for such cultural artifacts is therefore also a consequence of fallibility, and though the artifacts of culture may seem arbitrary to a purely logical observer, they fulfill very fundamental psychological needs of people. No matter how arbitrary the culture seems to logicians and epistemologists, individuals who participate actively in a culture tend not to feel any angst about philosophical fallibility and are more confident in moving through life. This also makes them more likely to succeed as entrepreneurs because of the link between culture and demand creation. In fact, every act of creating new demand is essentially adding a new cultural artifact to the culture and thus enriching and renewing the culture. After all, despite fallibility, we as individuals who have brains that hold thoughts are also part of the material universe, and that we exist is an indisputable part of our original agreement to assume the material universe is real. For Ramanuja, the Vedic dictum "Tat tvam asi" or "That! Thou art" means that after assuming the material universe is real, the next step is accepting that we as individuals are made of the same stuff that the material universe is made up of—and though we may never know the nature of reality completely, at any rate, we exist. In Western terms, the article of faith here is "I am, despite the fallibility of what I think" rather than Descartes' infallibilist illusion of "I think, therefore I am."

The journey of discovery of the nature of our desires and ourselves is part of the journey of discovering the nature of the material universe, though we are guaranteed through the incompleteness theorem that we will never reach the end of that discovery process. A large part of what we are as individuals with choice is determined by our cultural interactions with other individuals in a free and peaceful society, and the cultural artifacts we discover that we like and desire. Though new culture always stands upon the cultural artifacts of the past, a live culture must constantly update and renew itself and an ossification of culture purely into the immutable traditions of the past represents the death of culture itself, a consequential death of demand and desire, and a consequential death of the economy. It has historically always been the case that new innovations in cultures come in often by interaction with other cultures that are a source of ideas of what people may desire. This interaction and growth and assimilation of external culture is a very powerful way to increase the amount of live, new culture and discover people's desires without needing only research from first principles. No desire that does not violate the principle of non-coercion need be considered unsuitable for a culture—if an individual in a culture feels a desire, then it become a desire that belongs to that culture, regardless of whether the desire was first discovered in another culture and then was communicated. A society's desires can be nothing other than the sum of the desires of the individuals in that society, provided no desire that requires coercion of other individuals to satisfy is allowed or left legal by the society's government and private institutions.

Non-coercive demand stimulation: culture & demand

Now moving away from the philosophical realm, it is logically possible to imagine that an entrepreneur is creating demand person by person, but in practice it turns out that the only way an entrepreneur can create original demand is by contributing to the culture itself, and he will only succeed if a large enough number of people feel that it is compatible with their personalities. The sense of fallibility that pervades all individuals prevents most people from doing things radically at odds with what the people they respect and like are doing, even if some logical argument is made to them by some salesman. If sales and demand creation were only of the kind involving salesmen pulling wool over the customers' eyes and tricking him into a purchase, then it is unlikely capitalism would have thrived the way it has. In fact, most democratic countries have "anti-lemon" legislation, which allows customers to return a product within 30 days if they realize that they did not really want the product. In an economy with such legislation to prevent coercive and fraudulent sales, only genuine demand can exist. In other words, each individual has potential desires that can be discovered or actualized. It is an apparent truth that any free society that has progressed beyond subsistence is fundamentally engaged in discovering what desires it has in aggregate by allowing all individuals to freely discover what they desire. The role of the entrepreneur is not exactly someone creating desire out of a blank slate, which indeed would be something nearly impossible, but someone who helps individuals discover what potential desire they already had, by putting choices in front of them.

Indeed, examples of how innovation has discovered new demand exist in all modern economies. In the US, minority-owned businesses have uncovered huge opportunities in producing ethnic music, food, and entertainment—demand that did not exist earlier. In India in the 1990's,

Pepsi followed a culturally local branding campaign using local managers and local celebrity endorsements, while Coke followed an international branding campaign. Coke failed miserably while Pepsi thrived, and eventually Coke was forced to reverse their strategy. There is no law saying people who belonged to 'foreign' communities could not have produced these culture-entwined brands, but the fact is that demand creation and culture are highly inter-twined. To discover and actualize demand in any particular community, the entrepreneur must engage himself or herself completely with members of that community. This need not only refer to an ethnic community—for instance, to sell something to Chief Financial Officers (CFO's) of major companies, an entrepreneur needs to spend time with such CFO's and understand the culture and implicit epistemological assumptions that drive that sub-community of CFO's. He or she needs to be involved with the trade magazines and be able to contribute significant information of value to the magazine for distribution within the sub-culture. He or she needs to be present at the trade shows and gatherings of this community, and participate and add value and effort to community functions. Any entrepreneur who refuses to do those things is trying to be only an arbitrageur, and will probably suffer the Marxian fate of declining margins and imploding businesses because there is no cultural value being added. On the one hand, such cultural engagement allows potential customers to get to know the entrepreneur and trust him, but on the other hand, if the entrepreneur is unable to build such trust and cannot demonstrate any superior talents that he brings to the culture, he will not succeed in selling to the community. Branding and cultural participation practically guarantee a chance, but if what you are providing as an entrepreneur is not valuable you will still fail eventually and may destroy your credibility in the process.

The wisdom of commercial traditions

Thus we see there is great wisdom embedded in this practice of buying only from suppliers who are well-regarded in your community or one of the sub-communities you participate in. Despite fallibility of all theories, and the chance that someone with a slick story might convince you that their logic is the correct logic, this communitarian participation serves as a spontaneous safeguard against that fallibility. In all modern economies, all suppliers are asked for references, and such references are always checked. Price is never the sole determinant of a purchase, unlike the classical economists assumption, because fallibility cannot be ignored in a competitive marketplace. Although the first sale will always be the hardest, putting in the effort to participate in and contribute to a sub-culture will never fail to get that first chance to demonstrate your ability if at all you have anything of value to bring to that culture. The first sale and good references will then lead you to your next sales. Of course, value-for-money will always be a factor, and that is the basis of continuing productivity improvements in a free economy, so price is important but only within the context of the total value-for-money proposition, including the value of reduced risk of non-delivery of the product or service versus the risk with a competitor who does not spend the time or money, or part with information, to be involved at the face-to-face cultural level.

Coercion as entrepreneurial opportunity

One of the interesting aspects of Hayekian philosophy is that it becomes possible to view any pervasive act of coercion to represent an underlying entrepreneurial opportunity. Doing things coercively necessarily takes up more energy and economic resources than doing the same thing using voluntary participation. This is another point where Galbraith and Hayek, though from opposite poles of social thought, agreed. Galbraith too showed that power through psychological motivation in a corporation is far more efficient than coercion by force in primitive economies and inducement by high pay alone in mezzanine economies. Given that a non-coercive way of achieving certain objectives will be more economically efficient, an entrepreneur's task is now to find a way to place the option in front of the consumers in such a way that the habit of using the older coercive way gets changed to a habit of using the newer less coercive way. This theory, if true, brings to some concrete level Adam Smith's theory of an invisible hand that seems to inevitably bring better conditions for all citizens. However, it seems clear that such an invisible hand theory can only be true if the society is one that outlaws coercion of all kinds, rather than simply one that protects property rights. Property rights would also be protected under a coercion-banning regime, but so would rights of oppressed groups, religious minorities, powerless and uneducated workers, etc. The idea of fallibility and its consequence of a ban on coercion is a simpler and more powerful explanation than a dogmatic theory of property rights alone. In fact very little of Hayek's work discusses property rights explicitly, unlike most other classical-liberal economists and philosophers. As a result, Hayek is sometimes considered more a social scientist than an economist per se, but it would seem that that is an indictment of how economics is practiced today rather than Hayek's methodology, since economics is only one branch of social science that must be studied along with all other branches of social science including psychology, law, government, culture, ethics, and all other branches of human action, as Hayek's first teacher, Ludwig von Mises, has pointed out.

Branding

Though using macroeconomic and philosophical theory to determine where an entrepreneurial opportunity might lie can work, there is a large difference between spotting a theoretical opportunity and creating an organization and product that is known and trusted by people enough to actually spend the money and effort to buy the product. The first mistake to avoid is to avoid selling the industry or opportunity and focus exclusively on selling the product that is referenced by the brand name you choose to use. For instance, there is no point in starting a company to sell soap—you should instead sell "BrandX" or whatever name you choose to call your particular brand of soap. Not just generic soap. If you become a commodity supplier of soap or shoes or generic chemicals, then there is no hope of a sustainable business, and sooner or later Marx's declining profit theory will come to take its toll on you. Or to put it another way, if you see an arbitrage opportunity to produce generic unbranded products and make money, by all means seize the opportunity, but do not expect it to last and do not expect that anyone would ever buy the company from you for a large profit.

A lasting company is built by building a brand. All advantages and benefits you provide must be wrapped into the value proposition expressed by the word you use as a brand name. The relationship between you and your customers must always be a long term one that your customers perceive as valuable to them, and the brand name should over time come to mean all those things to them. You are inventing a new word in your sub-culture by creating a brand, and you will need to give depth of meaning to that word by actually providing and delivering certain benefits. Certainly you will have to provide some reliable product or service, but the issue of long-term importance is how you communicate that, how you incorporate that message into the word you use as your brand name, and how you continually strive to discover what your customers might like as additional value, and add that into your brand over time. There will be no end to this continual improvement and an end to evolution of a brand will also guarantee its death.

At all times, culture and brand will be inter-twined, but any number of sub-cultures may exist and each individual is usually considers themselves participants of more than one sub-culture. So you need to focus on which

sub-cultures you will target your brand and seek to participate and contribute to that sub-culture. For instance, to get a reputation of reliability,
you will need independent third-party validations of your product or service. Advertising serves only a limited purpose—the real brand building
value comes from un-coerced third-party opinions of you and your product. For this, you will need to interact with the people who run trade magazines and third-party testing laboratories in that field and educate them
about the features and benefits that you provide and have them validate it
and report on it. If you are the one setting up trade magazines, you will
have to interact with customers, organize trade shows and events, seek out
important new developments, test and review new products, etc. through
extensive interaction both with consumers and suppliers. Culture is about
interaction between people, about face-to-face meetings where you can
look at peoples eyes and shake their hands or use other such cultural traditions to help determine whether you are being lied to (coerced) or not.
Your supplier is as susceptible to fallibility as you are, and if he is lying, he
will be feeling fear and anxiety and you can possibly detect that. Culture is
about events that bring people together to interact freely instead of receiving possibly biased data streams. This helps them use subtle, culturally
specific, and yet unstated psychological techniques that we instinctively
use to determine the truth despite fallibility of our theoretical knowledge.

That art and entertainment is also part of culture means a two-way col-
laboration between those that provide pure art and entertainment, and
those that have capital budgets to spend on brand building. This interaction can be coercively misused, but if full disclosure is maintained, society
will discover the point at which the interaction leads to more mistrust
than trust, providing a spontaneous check on coercive use of the interaction, and only allowing the long term survival of providers of products
that are genuinely in demand and the providers of entertainment who are
genuinely liked. At this point, commerce and culture mutually reinforce
each other and provide constant non-coercive renewal and growth of both
culture and commerce.

Financing an enterprise

The key to accessing the credit markets for capital is proving a profitable business model and data supporting the creation of genuine demand. In a data-driven banking world, that would be sufficient to finance the capital needed to grow a business, since an entrepreneur could securitized future income and sell senior rights to that income to investors who provide capital up front. Of course, as of today securitization is still new and only a fraction of debt is securitized, so the ideal of 100% data-driven banking has yet to be achieved. Today, debt financing still depends on a banker who understands (or believes he understands) your business and feels that he trusts you or the collateral provided by co-signers on the loan. But in the near future, especially in advanced economies, proven data streams of income and profit will be immediately purchased into securitized pools and distributed to the capital markets. All an enterprise would need to do is to structure one's financial data in a format that a set of bonds can be created with senior and subordinate positions, and to make that data available to the capital markets. Such specific asset-backed debt would also typically be much cheaper than the current system of relationship-driven banking. A reference at the end of this book gives information about an online resource (co-founded by this author) which assists companies create such data trails and to potentially use that to access the securitized bond markets.

But even in advanced stages of securitized debt, the entrepreneur's first task is to raise the capital to start an experimental business before he has any track record of successful sales and income. For this, the only options are to first work for other companies and collect experience and savings, and to find a venture financier who will take equity risk along with your contribution to equity from savings in cash or through deferment of a full salary. Typically, such venture financiers will also look for a team of people who have gained experience in jobs with successful companies before financing them, in the absence of hard data of proven income. Entrepreneurs would therefore be best off first working for an established company for a period of time, and then starting a venture with a group of equal equity partners with complementary skills. It would be better to try solo ventures only after they have successfully started a company and then sold some shares to gain enough capital of their own so that they can employ the best professionals based just on salaries even if equal equity shares are not given. In developing countries this is sometimes not an option because of a lack of enough established ventures to gain experience from in the first place. I discuss this case in the last chapter on development economics.

Sustaining an enterprise

Fallibility is unrelenting. Even after a business has been started and run successfully, there are no guarantees that things will continue as they have in the past. The first step is obviously discovering what your customer finds valuable and delivering a complete solution to his needs, and continually refining that offering. During the whole time, you need to reinforce your brand and ensure that it communicates the entire value proposition that it offers using advertising as well as interacting with the press and sharing newly gained knowledge with the press and with customers. The press is certainly not going to take only your input and your competitors are sure to give them information as well, but you can take the competition as a source of knowledge too, and try to match their benefits and provide even more benefits.

Even so, many industries start off as brand new and then over time evolve and become very well known with not much new knowledge discovery forthcoming. At this point, entrepreneurs should always consider consolidation by merging with partners. Even in a crowded marketplace, if you have targeted specific niche cultures and markets and built a strong brand, you can command a premium for that bit of self-reinforced culture you have added to society. If yours is the dominant brand, you can raise more capital and buy other smaller and complementary brands. The main point is that though a company is an entrepreneur's creation, you must concentrate the value into the brand name and the long-term relationships that you can create with customers, and then be willing to sell the company at a point when your industry consolidates. The era of businesses owned by families for generations is long gone, and you would be doing a disservice to your heirs by encouraging them to join an old business when they could be participating and competing in new cultural events that will be at the core of the high-value opportunities of the future.

Management of large and growing organizations is another large topic that can benefit from acknowledgement of fallibility. The traditional business was autocratically run by the chief executive who had and used discretionary power arbitrarily, but modern businesses tend to be too complex and the market too competitive for this model to be sustained. A modern company needs several autonomous decision makers each focusing on a specialized role. The management techniques of Management By Objective, Deming's Total Quality Management (TQM), and Motorola's Six Sigma all represent one basic underlying principle—the articulation of the specific goals of each person in an organization and the assigning of a numerical metric by which the outcome is measured. After doing that, the individual responsible must take responsibility for finding the best method of how to achieve the targeted metrics. This method allows for decentralization of decision making without the top executive team trying to micro-manage all aspects of the business. The top executive in a well-implemented TQM system uses absolutely no coercion and simply steers the company by tweaking the particular numeric metrics that measure the performance of employees. Competition in this case can be accomplished by measuring achievements of peers against each other, as well as by encouraging continuous improvement, a process where individuals are forced to compete with their own past numeric achievements and constantly provide improvements over the previous period. Naturally, watching your competitors is also a staple part of trying to discover better and better ways of delivering value to your customers. Given fallibility, competition is actually good for all competitors in the sense that knowledge discovery is made more competitive and more experimental, and therefore more effective than simply trying to deduce the correct course of action through logic.

Services vs. manufacturing

It is worth looking at trends in sustainable business models in the face of a culture-brand theory of subjective value. Indeed, even if we look at the industrial development of Europe and America of the last 500 years, it is unclear whether the development was because it became cheaper to produce more material things using automation and technology, or because the public imagination was fired by the ideas of industrialization, creating more desires and hence economic demand. Having created the genuine demand, it simultaneously became sustainable to create capital through the engine of bank credit. But if this is so, then demand creation in the future need not be solely based on technological advances—any potential human desire can be researched and demand based on those desires can be actualized. Technology is still important because it would be impossible to competitively and profitably supply goods and services without using technology and knowledge of all kinds. But it is simply one of the tools used in both stimulating demand and satisfying it.

The act of actually manufacturing a product in the US today is a small fraction of the services that surround the product. Shoe manufacturers sell shoes for $100 a pair, but any number of companies in poorer countries offer to take up contracts to manufacture those same shoes at $2 a pair. But at the same time, the shoe company does not make $98 of profit. Instead, money is spent on design of the shoes, research into property of materials and manufacturing processes, investment in design and manufacture of manufacturing machines, advertising and marketing, sales and distribution, and financial services. After all these expenses, the shoe company struggles to make a 10% profit. If there were no low cost countries to actually manufacture the product at $2, there would no doubt be robotic machines that could be built that could build them, if not for $2, then perhaps for $10 a pair. Technology has reached a point where a manual labor job in manufacturing is not productive. The only reason robotic technology did not take off in the 1980's when it was technically advanced enough to do so, was because foreign trade with lower wage countries was able to provide the manual manufacturing cheaper than the cost of automation. Sooner or later, however, robotics will become cheaper than even the cost of subsistence of a person in any country, so manufacturing jobs are not likely to ever come back into vogue.

Other countries must therefore look at the approach taken by US companies in their plans for growth and change. Each culture needs to create its own brands, create marketing messages linked closely with targeted cultures and sub-cultures, create designs reflecting past culture and incorporating present trends, discover what sales and marketing techniques work in each sub-culture, and so on. Manufacture of the product can either be outsourced to countries that do not participate in this global self-discovery process, or be automated using robotic machines. A renaissance and renewal of local cultures in each place will also stimulate the third-party institutions needed to balance fallibility—magazines, newspapers, radio programs, and entertainment industries all need to be grown in and for each sub-culture. With modern global communications so advanced, each sub-culture can borrow what it needs from any other sub-culture in the world and discard parts it does not find useful. Only an infallibilist can view culture as something stagnant from the past and such infallibilist arguments are quite easily demolished by provable fallibility. A live culture consists of anything and everything that individuals in a society find desirable and do not involve coercion. Some of such live experimental culture will turn out to be ephemeral junk that is soon forgotten, but other parts will survive and evolve. It is also true that old habits are hard to break, so it follows that the types of new culture that most likely will be accepted by modern people will be culture that draws extensively on their own classical or ancient culture, but incorporates a modern reinterpretation of that culture. There is no doubt that ancient cultures, some if which have now become ossified, must originally have been such a cauldron of experimentation and exuberance rather than a fixed and immutable set of rules and regulations. In the face of fallibility, there is no other way culture could have emerged. But more jobs of far higher sustainable value will be created out of a constantly renewing cultural process and the process of stimulating demand, than could ever be created out of manufacturing widgets as sub-contractors for those who created demand in their own culture. There need be no concern of a shortage of capital once capital is seen as something that can be created and sustained as long as genuine demand exists.

New economics

To see the effect of a predominantly service-driven economy as opposed to a manufacturing-driven economy, we can use a tool provided by Hayek known as disaggregation. One of Hayek's concerns about a Keynesian approach to economics was the glorification of aggregate statistics. The economics profession uses assumptions of aggregate supply in the economy, aggregate demand, average period of production, average interest rate, aggregate supply of money and credit, etc. One of Hayek's contributions was to begin to disaggregate these aggregates in order to make more sense out of theory and bring theory closer to what actually happens in an economy.

Hayek starts with the period of production. It is fairly obvious from empirical observation that the banking system does not work on the premise of one single interest rate. If we disaggregate on the dimension of the period of production, we consider separately projects that need a loan for one year before repayment, two years, five years, ten years, and thirty years, for instance. When we look at the real economy we indeed see that the interest rate charged by banks varies depending on the period of production. In a bond market, this is known as the yield curve. The yield curve changes shape depending on the markets perception of where the economy is heading and provides key information to market participants and helps to make decisions on current and future investments. Since bonds in a market trade on a daily basis with any number of participants buying and selling, the yield curve at any point represents an inter-temporal (because it is never stable or static) consensus of all participants in the economy based on the individual experiences and knowledge of each of those participants. The knowledge embedded in the yield curve then is not knowledge created by the logical projections of a single centralized body, but a collective expression of the knowledge of several people, each with their own expertise and data points.

Aside from disaggregating on the dimension of the period of production, we can further use the Hayekian tool of disaggregation in the dimension of collateral type. In the asset-backed securitized bond market, the traded bonds are not just bond of a particular maturity but also of some particular collateral type. For instance residential mortgage-backed securities represent underlying residential home loans. Auto lease securities represent underlying auto loans. Each of these types of bonds of a variety of maturity periods trade every day in the markets. The market can continually express its collective opinion affecting not only the time-period based yield curve but also the yield expected for each type of collateralized loan. This again is superior to a single banker trying to figure out whether an industry is worth lending in using just logic and their own individual experience.

Another way of using disaggregation is to separate the cost of production of any good into the cost of manufacturing and the cost of demand stimulation, the latter including design, advertising, marketing, research, sales, distribution, financial services, etc.

$$Price = cost(production) + cost(demand) + profit$$

We can further assume that production costs are more heavily weighted toward material goods such as machinery and raw materials rather than labor, and demand creation costs are more weighted toward use of highly trained labor.

In industries where the cost of demand is relatively low, such as a purely export-oriented market, the business cycle can be fairly clearly predicted. Initially, when profit margins are high capital will flow in to create many companies to supply the demand. But eventually there would be too many companies and prices and profit margins would slowly tend toward zero.

Conversely, in industries where the cost of demand creation is the major cost such as a branded product or service, there would be no direct competition since each successful brand has sought out a differentiated niche in which it alone is positioned as the only or best option. In such an industry, the cost of actual production can be driven lower and lower by forcing any number of competing suppliers to bid for the contract to supply this demand which is owned by the brand owner. Although this can potentially increase the margins of the brand owner, constant reinvention and keeping up with changing patterns of desire will limit the brand owners profitability, but will create plenty of high paying jobs to provide the underlying services needed to create genuine quality of goods and services that can create genuine demand. An increase in population of such an economy can only be stimulative to it, adding demand, whereas an increase in population in an economy based solely on production as subcontractor to demand created by others will only create declining wages. Local culture in a production-oriented society would tend to become more and more neglected, being replaced by some sort of outward looking me-too caricature of the culture whose demand is being serviced rather than a discovery of what local people might desire.

The export trap

The production vs. demand orientation also will tend to affect global currencies. As returns on investment prove, as per Marxian theory, to become smaller and smaller in such production-oriented, export-oriented cultures, and as outlays on demand creation continue to rise, the currencies of export-oriented cultures will continue to decline, while the currencies of those cultures with active domestic demand creation engines would rise. Such a trend will become self-reinforcing since a depreciating currency will make exports more attractive, encouraging more capital investment in that direction, creating a further drain away from investments in domestic culture and demand. The trade surpluses that are created by exports will be more than dwarfed by the reverse flow of capital toward the economies with demand creation needs, destroying any chance of a trade surplus rescuing the currencies value. Current conventional wisdom that trade surpluses will cause currency appreciation and trade deficits will cause currency depreciation seems a perfect example of fallible theories—the incompleteness of the theory becomes apparent when we consider the volume of capital flows is far larger that trade flows and will always be the case since return on capital will always be less than the capital itself since capital can be manufactured freely through the instrument of credit expansion. Economies that are friendly toward inward capital investments will likely achieve currency appreciation regardless of their trade balance position.

While such exports should always be considered a legitimate arbitrage opportunity, such strategies will never be sustainable. Sooner or later a society will have to turn toward its own people and own culture and try to discover the desires and demands that can be satisfied for a profit. An open policy toward foreign capital can increase the amount of equity capital that flows in to finance new demand creation and demand discovery experiments, and such capital flows will enhance the value of the local currency, and through it the relative value of local culture and local demand.

EDUCATION

Discovery vs. teaching

People seem to dislike fallibility so much that the most effective way of convincing people of something seems to be to pretend to know it infallibly. To paraphrase an ancient saying, fallibility is like a well which many people wander around, but nobody goes into. Yet, it is not a source of fear at all when looked at in a rational perspective, but a beginning of true understanding of knowledge. Once we acknowledge that risk exists, we can start trying to manage it using data collection and free debate and tools of risk management. The worst denial of fallibility is to be found in modern institutions of learning. Institutions of learning that set up a fixed curriculum of instruction can never remain relevant. Instead, they need to teach a methodological explanation of how to set about discovering what is true. Even if the most knowledgeable people at a particular time set down in writing all their knowledge, in all likelihood the knowledge that is of any value would have changed by the time the writing was complete. This is especially true in modern times where change occurs faster than ever before in history, and it is increasingly obvious that what we learn in institutions of formal learning do not really play a role in how we find ways of making a living.

The meta-knowledge problem

At the core of the education problem then is a lack of knowledge about what knowledge is currently valuable. This meta-knowledge is particularly fallible, if knowledge itself is fallible. Though in modern democratic countries there is no explicit ban on people going wherever they want to learn whatever they want, there is still a meta-knowledge problem with three dimensions:

- How to know what skills and knowledge is currently valuable

- How to know who is an effective provider of those skills and knowledge

- How to know who would provide the financing that may be necessary to invest in that training.

People born in communities that have traditionally not been under-privileged tend to have informal networks that help navigate this problem, though not always in a completely effective way. People in under-privileged social groups have very little chances of navigating this issue at all. Before considering basic children's education, it is easier to look at the problem of adult education and re-training, especially in the context of changing technological environments that render old skills obsolete at an ever-increasing rate of change. The meta-knowledge problem in this case can be considered a type of market failure—there would be demand for information about the effectiveness of all training schools, but the market fails to supply such information since no one institution would want to be accountable unless all competing institutions were also similarly accountable.

At-risk student loans

A possible solution to the meta-knowledge problem in adult training is to set up an infrastructure where numeric data can be collected on the outcome vs. the desired outcome—i.e., the average income or increased income of people who graduate from various training courses. In addition, the burden of effectiveness of training can be shifted to the provider of the training by introducing the concept of an at-risk student loan. With at-risk loans, the provider of training does not charge the course fee up front, but instead provides a loan for the amount of the published fee, but will take repayments only as a percentage of income above a certain projected minimum income expected for a graduate of the course. If the student's income does not exceed that level, the loan would not have to be paid back. It is easy to see that if a provider of training is willing to take such responsibility for the income result of training, it will also be possible for them to charge much more in fees that they currently charge, as long as they are effective in achieving the needed return on investment. They may then also be able to invest in more training infrastructure and much higher salaries for teachers who have more relevant and valuable skills or are better at creating material for instruction in such knowledge.

Knowledge Backed Securities

In order to manage the risks involved in such at-risk loans, the training school can use the most amazing financial innovation in history—securitization. By creating a waterfall of senior and subordinate tranches of a pool of at-risk loans given to students, training schools can sell off senior tranches to the capital markets. All that would be needed is statistical data of past performance of the school. Even if, as will inevitably happen, some percentage of students turn out to be incapable of getting employment at the targeted wages, this percentage can be written-off as the subordinate or equity tranche of the pool of loans, but the returns on the remaining loans in the pool would be sufficient to make up the loss.

Naturally, care would have to be taken that students do not misuse the system by taking the course and then disappearing. Again, the system for preventing this cannot be via central control but by introducing disincentives for doing that so that students regulate themselves. For instance, this can be accomplished by encouraging employers to check the references and course scores of an employee by accessing the online records of the training school. At this point, the employer would get to now whether the employee is a defaulter on his student loan. This creates a disincentive for a student to default, and given that he or she need not pay back the loan if they do not earn, there should really be no reason for an honest student to disappear from the reach of the training school. Indeed, the system of consumer credit in the US makes use of exactly this form of spontaneous incentive for people to pay back their loans. The US consumer credit markets, incidentally, are one of the biggest users of securitization as a vehicle to finance and manage consumer debt. The data on consumer credit-worthiness itself has proven to be a valuable economic asset in itself and would more than pay back on the infrastructure and technology needed to collect and maintain the data. The same would apply to data on the economic performance of people who take various courses. The data can also be aggregated, or otherwise be made anonymous, and disclosed to new potential students looking to upgrade their skills. Though no school could or would ever have infallible ways of knowing what training would be effective, competitive discovery would ensure that the society as a whole would continually discover and re-discover what training it takes to add economic value in a changing economy.

Once we see how securitized at-risk loans brings data, accountability, and discovery to the education system, it is worth re-looking at the concept of money supply expansion through the instrument of credit. We noted earlier in the chapter on money and banking that the way to prevent general unproductive inflation in prices was to ensure that the quality of lending is good rather than simplistically looking at the quantity of money supply growth. This is particularly relevant for the at-risk training industry. As long as training schools maintain the data of their effectiveness, there need be no quantitative limit on creating credit for training. As much money as is needed by the economy can be created by the banking system, as long as all the securitized bonds are traded publicly so that the market keeps a spontaneous check on the quality, effectiveness, and productivity of capital. With such securitized at-risk training loans—what we might call Knowledge Backed Securities—there will therefore be no conceivable resource problems normally associated with education when we think of government funding of such education using a limited tax revenue base. The analysis and confrontation of fallibility has then helped us to identify the risks and set up self-monitoring systems for people to discover the best way forward given the collective experience of all players in the market. This is not a solution that we are discussing here, but simply a way that we might have a chance of discovering the solution, or rather, a diverse set of solutions, to the education problem despite the essential fallibility of our knowledge.

Basic education

Children's education is less about learning economically valuable knowledge than having a safe and nurturing environment where the natural abilities of imagination can fully develop. Imagination, if suppressed at a young age, is very hard to learn later. Nevertheless, there can be yet undiscovered ways of providing such an environment and basic skills such as reading, writing, arithmetic, logic, history, geography, music, sport, social skills, etc. One way of introducing competition suggested by Milton Friedman and endorsed by Hayek is for the government to provide vouchers to parents who would then choose which school to send their children too. But this is unaffordable for developing countries, and does not particularly solve the meta-knowledge problem for parents who are disadvantaged in the first place and may not have the cultural networks that know which schools are the best. A better way would be to replicate the US system for college education—the government has set up a securitization trust called Sallie Mae that underwrites college loans, securitizes them, and sells them to the capital markets. The idea is on the right track but the mistake is that the US government set up a monopoly institution to do this. It should rather encourage private competitive securitization trusts that would work hard at discovering which colleges are effective and which are not. The government could restrict itself by providing re-insurance to a certain portion of the equity tranche in the securitization, and over time may not even need to do that. An equivalent of Sallie Mae for basic education for children would ensure that the funding provided for education would be returned if and when the student grows up and earns income, and re-used for funding the next generation of children. This could be done both in rich countries as well as developing countries, though the proportion of government provided insurance in poor countries would probably need to be higher. Since the burden will be borne by the currency rather than the fiscal budget, there is no country that cannot afford such universal competitive education.

DEVELOPMENT ECONOMICS

Hyperinflation in agro-money

As we discussed earlier, agrarian and developing economies face a different challenge from those that spent centuries transitioning from agrarian to industrial and then to service economies. In agrarian economies, very often grain itself is one of the currencies in circulation. In rural India, for instance, a poor villager may have no income sources, but might still be able to grow some grain and barter some grain for some cooking oil, salt, and vegetables. But when technologies have made the supply of food-grain suddenly much larger that it was before, the value of the grain as a currency correspondingly depreciates. For the agrarian villager, it is the equivalent of hyperinflation in the prices of goods he was accustomed to buying using grain that he grew. So far, India and other similar countries have maintained controls over food import and have artificially controlled food-grain prices. But such moves have had the inevitable side effects on productivity, essentially providing an incentive for people dependent on agriculture to remain dependent on agriculture rather than learning some new skill. Needless to say, in the absence of some scheme of solving the meta-knowledge problem, it is not clear whether they would have been able to learn new skills even if the government had not interfered with market forces. There may well have been mass-starvation or violent rebellion had the government controls been removed and the meta-knowledge problem left unresolved.

Securitized first aid

So rather that focus on whether the past government responses to rapid changes in the relative value of knowledge were appropriate, we might instead try to anticipate the knowledge problem and the welfare problem and formulate ways in which we might discover paths toward a more productive future. In the first place, a structure such as Knowledge Backed Securities would need to be created and tested. But since it is unlikely that all people are likely to be able to be retrained and employed immediately, there is also some cause to call for a negative income tax such as the 17th century Poor Law in England, as Hayek suggested. But since poor countries cannot afford such extensive expenses, an alternative strategy would be to provide such minimum income guarantees as loans, and to provide them via training schools that provide retraining so that all people receiving such assistance are also receiving new skills training so that the need for assistance will disappear over time. Such welfare loans can be created by any government no matter what resources it has, since this is credit money that is being created. The burden is taken by the currency rather than the fiscal budget. Such handouts would also have the effect of stimulating local demand, and creating an opportunity for entrepreneurs to supply that demand in a way consistent with the desires of each local community. The only thing to be careful of is that all loans should be securitized and traded publicly so that the market will demand disclosure of data and ensure spontaneous monitoring of training school performance.

Private currencies

Traditional currencies in developing countries are usually weighed down by non-transparent non-accountable loans. As an alternative to waiting for regulations and restructuring to take place through government action, it is possible for private groups to create their own synthetic units of accounts, and start creating competitive money supply through loans that are collateralized by some asset. Ideally, a single global unit of account residing on a coordinated information system is desirable, but many independent information systems and synthetic units of account are also possible. The market will probably invent some means of interchanging such currencies before long, anyway, since an asset is an asset and there will be people willing to pay something for it, based on the history of yield on that asset. But the upshot of this is that the theories can even be tested on small isolated regions by creating a local synthetic currency and allowing only asset backed loans to be created by an unlimited number of banking participants. Development experiments can then be conducted in various places, and best practices will tend to spread around spontaneously, aided by accountable training schools that teach best practices.

Training entrepreneurs

The training schools that would likely be most effective would be those that develop the theories and practices of entrepreneurship most effectively. The Hayekian discussions in this book might provide some insight, but they are surely incomplete. The discovery process may be long and difficult in each local community, but by commitment to discovery rather than looking for infallible teachers to show us how to thrive, we will have a better chance of discovering the effective methods of entrepreneurship.

Such entrepreneurship schools could also provide micro-venture capital as at-risk loans in addition to paying for the fees and for basic subsistence. Indeed, such experiments have already proven successful following a brilliant experiment by the Grameen Bank, initially in Bangladesh and now used in many developing countries by many banks. But the Grameen Bank and other micro-loan projects have not really used the tool of securitization.

Securitization has historically been restricted to loans involving massive amounts of capital, often because the amount of information technology and research needed to do a deal is prohibitively expensive. But new automated software tools for managing securitization deals—such as the one referenced in the Bibliography of this book—makes the cost of deal engineering and deal management much lower, and democratizes the tool of securitization. By using securitization, even micro-credit programs can become more knowledge-efficient and manage risk at a low enough cost.

Epistemology for venture capitalists

This knowledge management aspect of securitization is far more important than the traditional role of securitization used just to unload assets from a bank's portfolio. It no longer becomes necessary to know exactly what projects will work—simply fund a large number and study the data to see which ones should be further funded and which ones should be allowed to close down if unprofitable. By securitizing the investments, the risks can be managed and the net profit can still be expected to be positive. During the process we would discover what types of businesses are compatible and sustainable within each culture.

By securitizing venture capital of all kinds—from small micro-loans to mid-size and large-scale projects—even the risks involved in venture capital can be managed. For instance, if a venture capital provides $100 million in financing to various ventures, and then creates a $50 million senior tranche of that which will take the first 25% of any profits, they could easily sell off the $50 million senior tranche to investors who want the potential of high return, but want some isolation from the risks. Any number of such tranches can be created to separate various types of risks and provide different levels of risk exposure and reward potential. Even retail investors may prefer to invest in securitized tranches of pools of equities—publicly traded or private—so that they do not have to have infallible prescience in order to know which stock to invest in. Securitization of venture capital is probably essential in developing economies where culturally specific demand is yet to be discovered, but it is also a tool to protect against fallibility for any venture capitalist in any economy. Too often, we see venture capitalists who have a "strategy" and who claim they "know" exactly what types of businesses will work. A venture capitalist that studies a little Hayekian epistemology should instead know that his theories would always be fallible. To guard against fallibility, the precise thing to avoid is particular strategies of focus rather than simply trying to find entrepreneurs who understand their businesses better than the venture capitalist ever can, and diversifying risk at a different level by broadening the types of investments made.

Securitization then is the precise knowledge management and risk management tool that is needed to manage fallibility. The reason it works is the reason most of science works—it focuses heavily on data from all possible sources and allows different, competitive interpretations of the data. Relying on data does not guarantee infallible theories, but given the assumption that the material universe exists and supplies us with data about its nature, what we need to do is allow competitive theories to battle it out so that we discover the ones that are most accurate. And while incorrect theories still remain, we can minimize risk by pooling risks and splitting them out in different ways so that those willing to take risk can take it, and those who cannot yet afford to take risk can find shelter. There is still no guarantee that all these techniques will solve the problems of fast-changing technology-intensive global society, but at least they provide a technique for making progress and learning from both mistakes and successes.

Appendix I
A Rationalist's Guide to Religion

The second half of the second millennium AD was driven by a profound change in people's attitude to religion. Prior to that era, practically everyone in the world believed in some religion and some form of God. But with the advance of science, logic, and technology, man was suddenly able to accomplish results that seemed to be at odds with prior notions of how an individual's will cannot be achieved, and "God's will" would prevail. Descartes' geometry and rationalism became the poster child for the new age of reason, where religion would be treated as the enemy of truth and enlightenment. There was much evidence to suggest that religions were indeed guilty as charged—senseless wars and crusades were commissioned by heads of religious communities, priests abused their power over their flock in order to make a luxurious living, and tribal notions of the role of women, slaves, and unbelievers were perpetuated by conflating the power of religion with the personal predilections of the all-too-human priests and community leaders.

In the 21st century, the reaction to all these religion-inspired abuses seems to fall into two broad categories—those who profess to be agnostic or atheists, and those who claim to be 'spiritual' but not a part of any organized religion. Both camps generally do believe in the power and utility of reason. But there is still a gap between rationalism and the worldview of traditionally religious people. I attempt to bridge this gap and provide a rational explanation for many of the sayings found in all of the major world religions including Christianity, Islam, Judaism, Hinduism, and Buddhism. I try to show that there is an interpretation of religious words and beliefs that is different from how the professedly religious criminals interpreted their own religious texts.

First, we must summarize the precepts of a rationalism that accepts fallibility. In the preceding pages we used simple deduction to establish the following basic theories that seem to be irrefutable.

Theorem 1: *All theories are based on an incomplete set of facts.*

Theorem 2: *As a consequence of Theorem 1, all theories are fallible.*

This necessitates an assumption of **Axiom 0:** *Despite our fallibility of our inferences, we will assume the material universe exists and gives us valid data via our perceptions.* Although this is intuitively obvious, the provable fallibility of knowledge implies that we must formally call this an assumption in which we must have faith. We will continue to use this assumption until and unless it is refuted.

Theorem 3: *Since justifications for violence or coercion are fallible, morality is defined by a ban on coercion and fraud. The purpose of law is to detail the various forms of coercion and formally outlaw each type.*

Theorem 4: *Due to provable fallibility, institutions of law must follow due process and presumption of innocence while enforcing a ban on coercion.*

Theorem 5: *Democracy is a process by which people who are coerced can express such coercion and seek resolution. Without democracy, fallibility and inherent power structures will not allow feedback of the coercion of the powerless.*

Theorem 6: *Discovery of valid theories about the nature of material reality is best achieved by critique of competitive theories, often resulting in synthesizing a new theory that encompasses the facts earlier ignored by each of the preceding theories.*

Theorem 7: *Allowing complete freedom of action other than those actions that involve coercion or fraud will accelerate the discovery of valid theories.*

Theorem 8: *Competitive trading of bank loans will most efficiently discover the business areas that work.*

Theorem 9: *Competitive funding of student loans and adult re-skilling loans will achieve the most rapid and effective training of individuals so that they may increase their wealth even in rapidly changing technological environments.*

Theorem 10: *Basic welfare through food stamp loans for the indigent will not distort the knowledge discovery process of free and competitive innovation. With basic food and nutrition security guaranteed, adult training will provide a path for economic development of all without continued subsidies.*

Given these ten theorems and the accompanying axiom, all of which should be acceptable to a rationalist, we will now take a look at the precepts of various religions. To be sure, we will omit several precepts that the religions do have, but let us keep in mind that the original message of religions may have been altered or added to by theologians who may have misunderstood their own faith. I only claim that there is enough in each religion to find common ground between rationalism and religion.

Hinduism and Buddhism

It is worth discussing Hinduism first here, since it is perceived to be polytheistic. In actual fact, Hinduism is monotheistic and uses the name *Brahman* to denote the notion of the one God. All other 'gods' in the Hindu pantheon are considered only aspects of the one *Brahman*. Modern Hinduism is actually a revivalist movement that began in the 8th century AD, before which Buddhism had largely replaced Hinduism in the Indian subcontinent. The founder of the revivalist movement was Sankara, who in the 8th century AD walked across the country explaining his interpretation of the near-extinct knowledge contained in the Vedas, an interpretation he named *Advaita* or Non-Dualism, which is the central concept in the Vedas. He set up four centers for scholarly research into the Vedas, which over the next 400 years were the driving force behind the Hindu revival. In the 11th century, however, Sri Ramanuja overturned the conventional Sankara interpretation of the Vedas and offered an entirely new way of interpreting the Vedas, which he called *Visista Advaita* or "A Special Theory of Non-Dualism". The main difference was the definition of truth. According to Sankara, the concept of *Maya* means that material reality is an illusion and it does not really exist. Accordingly, he claimed that the concept of *Brahman* or ultimate reality was equated to enlightened human consciousness. God, or *Brahman*, was a human-like entity, but one which any human could become one with through attaining enlightenment. Ramanuja found this interpretation entirely inadequate. He defines the word 'God' by saying "the material universe is the body of God." For the rationalist, this implies that saying "God exists" is no more adventurous than saying "material reality exists." For Ramanuja, *Maya* then refers to the fact that human interpretations of our perceptions are fallible. But despite the fallibility, we must assume that the material universe is real—i.e. we must have faith that the material universe exists, that

'God' exists. This corresponds exactly to the rational deductions we make using incompleteness, fallibility, and logic.

Ramanuja went on to make various other interpretations of the Vedas using the twin axioms that the material universe is real, but our inferences are fallible. He explained the difference between *vidya*, or knowledge, and *sat*, or truth. Truth is what exists—the material universe. Knowledge is our interpretations of our perceptions of the truth, of reality. But each theory we have may be true—*sat*—or false—*asat*. Holding a false belief is therefore described as *avidya*. To discriminate between *vidya* and *avidya*, Ramanuja recommended the tool of criticism or discrimination. He said that though 'God'—the material universe—was only one, it is not homogenous. In fact, God (reality) is infinitely variegated and the human brain is a device that in essence is one capable of perceiving differences. Words are what we assign to the perceived differences, and language evolves based on ever finer perceptions of difference.

The other major departure from Sankara's interpretations was in the interpretation of the Vedic phrase "*Tat tvam asi*" or "That! Thou art!" The post-Sankara mainstream of Hinduism interprets that to mean that the individual consciousness is God—that consciousness precedes material existence. Ramanuja turned that on its head and said it just means that we as individuals also exist in the material world, and therefore we a part of God (material reality)—we are not everything God is, but since we materially exist, we are a part of God. But human beings—or any sentient beings that have a perception engine such as the brain and use it to develop language—are surely a special or divine part of reality. Sentience is therefore something that has degrees—even animals have a brain and perceive reality, but they do not have language. The ultimate degree of sentience is a being that realizes that they are using a brain and language and understands the relationship between reality (*sat*) and knowledge (*vidya*) about reality. The phrase "*Aham Brahman*" or "I am (a part of) Brahman/God" affirms the importance and uniqueness of sentience (*chit*) as distinct from the insentient (*achit*).

The Buddhist derivatives of Hinduism use the concept of fallibility to detach a person from material needs. But Hinduism reiterates in the Bhagvad Gita that though one need not be overly attached to anything, this does not mean that enlightenment will come through pure detached meditation. It is only by engaging reality and interacting with it that one can understand the truth of the fallibility of one's knowledge and will and the supremacy of material reality. Reading words and ignoring material reality is insufficient and can only lead to misinterpretations. One must exercise one's free and fallible will and see which of the things we will are consistent with reality and which ones have adverse and unanticipated consequences. Each person then finds a unique and personal path to enlightenment that is best suited for the experiences and situations faced by that person. But given incompleteness and fallibility, there may be many things that a person wills but is unable to achieve—in the face of this, one can use the techniques of detachment to accept that reality has its own way and one might instead turn away from achievements and simply contemplate the many wonderful aspects of reality and nature.

In the face of fallibility, free will is also the method by which people can build a culture and society that is sustainable. Here is where the concept of non-violence—*ahimsa*—comes into play. Actions that do not coerce another sentient individual do not have adverse consequences. Such non-coercive free actions that become popular and imitated form the basis of a culture, and a means to prosperity and richness in life. Conversely, any act of coercion against another individual has adverse consequences (adverse *karma*). Thus natural law (*dharma*) is based on the varied consequences of a ban on coercion. As society becomes more complex, new laws can be discerned by using the principle that coercion is what needs to be allowed, but free will must be given full reign beyond that restriction. But note that the law (*dharma*) is discerned from critically observing the nature of reality—not decided arbitrarily by a fallible individual or group.

Judaism and Christianity

Turning now to Christianity, the key aspect for the rationalist reader is to see that Jesus was speaking of what he felt was the correct interpretation of Jewish scripture. That is, he was not negating that God/reality drove Abraham and Moses to speak what they discerned to be the truth, but simply saying that the popular interpretations at the time were incorrect in some ways. He acknowledged that it was the same God that he was speaking of. Now if we see that material reality is that 'God' then it is not irrational at all to agree that they were all talking about the same source of knowledge—material reality had always been there and was still there and would always be there and its basic nature had not changed and will never change.

The New Testament of the Bible is best understood as a set of theses written about what Jesus was talking about. Given that these were written by fallible human beings, one can expect that there are misinterpretations of what it was that Jesus was actually talking about. For instance, if material reality is what is meant by the term 'God', then it is not unreasonable to assert that God exists, and only one God exists. Many of the other phrases attributed to Jesus can also be reinterpreted using the concepts of material reality as God and human knowledge as fallible interpretations of perceptions of reality. The gospel of St. Thomas is one such source of phrases attributed to Jesus—that this gospel by one of the apostles of Jesus was left out of the Bible is one consequence of the difficulty that people faced interpreting Jesus' words. Didymos Judas Thomas was known as the doubting Thomas after all, so it is not unreasonable to assume he was the best critical thinker among Jesus' followers. His gospel contains some sayings that are in other gospels and others that are missing. Here are some of them with the rational fallibilistic interpretations:

> Jesus said, "If your leaders say to you, 'Look, the (Father's) kingdom is in the sky,' then the birds of the sky will precede

you. If they say to you, 'It is in the sea,' then the fish will precede you. Rather, the kingdom is within you and it is outside
you. When you know yourselves, then you will be known, and
you will understand that you are children of the living Father.
But if you do not know yourselves, then you live in poverty,
and you are the poverty."

Given the definition of God as the whole of material reality, this is a
very obvious statement. The 'kingdom' of God' is not elsewhere—it is
everywhere within us and around us. When we know ourselves—that our
knowledge is fallible due to the nature of our brain, perception, and language—then we will understand that we are part of reality (children of the
Father). If we do not know ourselves—if we think our opinions are infallible—then it will lead us to many acts of coercion against others and ultimately ourselves.

Jesus said, "The person old in days won't hesitate to ask a little
child seven days old about the place of life, and that person
will live. For many of the first will be last, and will become a
single one."

Again, the fallibility of knowledge is a lifelong fact. Yet since material
reality is real, the perceptions of everyone, including a small child, are
important and contains information about reality. It behooves even the
wisest man to ask the most ignorant what their opinions are. After all,
those opinions are there because of the impressions created on that mind
by some aspects of reality that the wise man may have missed. By asking
and questioning, the wise man can find out ever more about reality/God.

Jesus said to his disciples, "Compare me to something and tell
me what I am like."

Simon Peter said to him, "You are like a just messenger."

Matthew said to him, "You are like a wise philosopher."

Thomas said to him, "Teacher, my mouth is utterly unable to say what you are like."

Jesus said, "I am not your teacher. Because you have drunk, you have become intoxicated from the bubbling spring that I have tended."

And he took him, and withdrew, and spoke three sayings to him. When Thomas came back to his friends they asked him, "What did Jesus say to you?"

Thomas said to them, "If I tell you one of the sayings he spoke to me, you will pick up rocks and stone me, and fire will come from the rocks and devour you."

This is an interesting story of why Jesus may not have been able to speak as plainly in the logic and materiality that is commonplace today. The worldview of people in that region in those days was such that they may have simply gone insane hearing that reality was God. What Jesus may have been trying to do is speak about fallibility and materiality in terms that were well understood and taken for granted in that community at that time. He also is clear that it is not him that is teaching—he is trying to say that reality will teach all those who accept it and engage it. Actions have consequences, and in living them out we will always learn the same lessons in every age past and every age to come.

Jesus said, "You see the sliver in your friend's eye, but you don't see the timber in your own eye. When you take the timber out of your own eye, then you will see well enough to remove the sliver from your friend's eye."

Again, this becomes clear when we consider fallibility. Until we recognize that our own opinions are fallible, we cannot remove any infallibilist illusion that our friends are suffering from.

Jesus said, "I took my stand in the midst of the world, and in flesh I appeared to them. I found them all drunk, and I did not find any of them thirsty. My soul ached for the children of humanity, because they are blind in their hearts and do not see, for they came into the world empty, and they also seek to depart from the world empty. But meanwhile they are drunk. When they shake off their wine, then they will change their ways."

The human mind finds it hard to absorb the lesson of its own fallibility. It is not interested in learning about fallibility. The brain is chemically addicted to knowing with certainty, and it does not listen easily to those who claim otherwise. People are in that sense drunk. When they awaken and realize the fallibility of their opinions, they will cease to coerce others.

Jesus said, "If the flesh came into being because of spirit, that is a marvel, but if spirit came into being because of the body, that is a marvel of marvels. Yet I marvel at how this great wealth has come to dwell in this poverty."

This is a direct comment that reality precedes consciousness. When a person finally realizes that the material is primary and starts to study reality, including people, with humility, then it is surely a marvel. Yet we are unwilling to accept this basic truth and dwell in the consequences of the coercive acts that we justify to ourselves as necessary.

Jesus said, "The Pharisees and the scholars have taken the keys of knowledge and have hidden them. They have not entered nor have they allowed those who want to enter to do so."

This is a comment that attacks the institutions that spring up after anyone successfully preaches the consequences of fallibility. The priests who seek power convert it into an anthropomorphic god and place themselves as the knowers of true and infallible knowledge. They will not enter the enlightenment of fallible rationalism and will not allow others to either.

His disciples said to him, "When will the rest for the dead take place, and when will the new world come?" He said to them, "What you are looking forward to has come, but you don't know it."

This is again the denial of heaven as some place other than the material reality we are already in. We only need to realize it.

Jesus said, "Congratulations to the poor, for to you belongs Heaven's kingdom."

This is an insight that people who are poor know intimately that their knowledge is fallible and that material reality is real. Wealthy and powerful people do not easily recognize this because their will is often achieved, and often at the cost of known or unknown coercion.

Jesus said, "Whoever has come to know the world has discovered the body, and whoever has discovered the body, of that one the world is not worthy."

Again, the assertion that discovery of the nature of material reality and our own physical and mental nature is true enlightenment. But it is thankless in a world of people who are drunk on infallibilist opinions.

Simon Peter said to them, "Make Mary leave us, for females don't deserve life." Jesus said, "Look, I will guide her to make her male, so that she too may become a living spirit resembling you males. For every female who makes herself male will enter the kingdom of Heaven."

This is a surprising bit of modern gender equality for its time. A traditional woman could remain sheltered in false security of assuming her opinions are infallible as long as there was a man who protected her and remained vigilant to unexpected events in an uncertain world. But when women choose to become 'men', or in other words to shoulder the responsibilities one has to in negotiating an uncertain world on one's own, to take risks and still act without coercing others, then she becomes as enlightened in all respects.

There are many more parts of the gospel, and over time it ought to be possible to find an interpretation for many of them in the light of fallible materiality, and to dismiss some of them as the misinterpretations due to the all too human weaknesses of the writers. But there is sufficient similarity to suggest that experience in the real world was what led the Jewish and Christian prophets to say what they did in the context of their times. The definition of the word 'God' as material reality itself brings rationality to vast tracts of mystical writing.

Islam

Turning now to Islam, we first need to decide which of the writings to look most closely at. Islam has two primary sources of knowledge—the Koran, which is the word of God as spoken to Mohammed, and the Hadith which is the narration of the life of Mohammed as told by various priests after Mohammed's death. Clearly, as in the vedic and biblical analysis above, we can expect many mistakes and coercive intrusions of fallible human opinion in the Hadith, and can therefore focus on the words that Mohammed claimed were of God/truth/reality. But it is also true that the Hadith contains many wise sayings. But even a faith-based logic dictates that in order to infer which of them are correct and which incorrect, one would have to critically examine them and eliminate any that contradict the core words of the Koran itself. Indeed, in all the Muslim countries prior to the invasion of Crusaders from Europe, there was freedom of worship for all faiths, free debate on all issues, due process in law, and respect for individual freedom. Faith in the Koran was expected only by choice and not by force.

The central tenet of Islam is the same one as fallibilistic rationalism—i.e., that human knowledge is fallible. The reasoning from there leads to all the same conclusions of modern liberalism that we discussed in the theorems at the beginning of this essay. The Koran contains many exhortations to retain faith that God's will is what is true and individual will is fallible. It says that those who persist in infallibilist illusions will come to a bad end. But like any religion, and especially after the trauma of massive and bloody invasions from Europe in the Middle Ages, power tends to get usurped by priests who would be dictators and who imagine they have infallible knowledge. With Islam, it is ironical that they hold up the very book that emphasizes the fallibility of the individual while asserting that their word is law.

The second plank of Islam is the emphasis on ethics. It is not considered permissible for a Muslim to act unethically. Now, the issue is reconciling this second tenet of Islam with its first, namely, that knowledge is fallible. If one goes by the Hadith which currently includes both wise and foolish statements, and conclude that only life in full accordance with the Hadith is ethical, and all other acts are unethical, then we would be relying on the words and actions of fallible men rather than the word of God as per Mohammed. But like the other religions and modern liberalism, Islam concurs that coercion of any individual is wrong. This definition of ethics as full freedom of action other than coercing other individuals is one that is compatible with all religious "words of God" and yet can be justified purely rationally as well.

Islamic law in the Middle Ages was extremely cognizant of fallibility and was faithful to presumption of innocence and due process for all. Modern nominally Islamic dictatorships are actually not in line with either of these two basic tenets of Islam and its dictators are possessed by their own infallibilist illusions—in Islamic terms they are in the grip of the devil and not God.

The third plank of Islam, like Christianity in some respects, is the absolute necessity for basic welfare. Abject poverty is considered completely unacceptable and against everything that is holy. But while this is achieved through charity in Islamic societies, it also leads to a concentration of power that can distort the market discovery process. With food stamp loans run by a democratic government, the same outcome of basic welfare can be achieved along with a preservation of competitive discovery of ever more productive techniques.

One of the aspects of Islam that is relevant to modern liberalism is its treatment of banking. It holds that banking with unlimited liability of the borrower is unethical. Instead, an aspect Islamic banking called *salam* allows a form of lending that attaches particular asset collateral. The risk of default is then carried by the named asset alone, and not the entire savings and assets of the borrower. For instance, a farmer can sell part of next year's crop at a discount to the expected market value of the crop. If the crop fails, the creditor must absorb the loss. This is identical to the modern asset backed securitization market in banking. If a homeowner defaults on a mortgage he will lose the house, but will get any extra proceeds from the sale of the house after paying back the lender. Asset backed lending, as discussed in the main section of this manuscript, is therefore completely compatible with the tenets of Islamic banking ethics, and in fact was practiced throughout the Muslim world even in the days of Mohammed. And as discussed in the book, asset backed banking is data driven rather than relationship driven—anyone meeting the criteria will get the loan, not just the cronies of the individual banker. This discretion is the main source of unethical behavior in modern banking, and its decline actually increases the safety of the banking and monetary system by using data to ensure that the quality of loans made is high.

The last remaining aspect of Islam that is relevant to this discussion is education. Education is highly valued in Islamic countries. In the early days of Islam before the Crusades, education was liberal and allowed dissenting views, debates, and participation of scholars from all faiths. Muslim countries were the ones who preserved the Greek classics of Socrates, Aristotle, Plato, and the others. Without this preservation, and its retrieval by secret societies from among the Crusaders, the Western Enlightenment and the resulting liberalism and scientific progress could never have taken place. But in order to retain an education system that constantly questions conventional wisdom and seeks out ever better theories of reality, competition is essential. The system of securitized education loans that are traded publicly therefore is the one that would be consistent with the central tenet of fallibility in Islam. Education loans too are essentially asset-backed loans, where the asset is the knowledge that is imparted to the individual. If the knowledge were good, then the person would be able to earn enough to pay back the loan. Otherwise, the creditor would have to bear the loss. Since the responsibility for loan quality is on creditors who are successful competitors, quality of loans will be higher because they are in a better position than the ignorant student on which training courses to fund.

Thus the central tenets of Islam of fallibility, ethics, welfare, ethical banking, and education are all tenets that are compatible with modern liberalism. Combined with the discussions of material reality as God in order to make sense of religious writings, and the insights of other religions from Hinduism to Christianity, there is a compelling case for modern rationalists to understand religion in a way that was for a long while unthinkable. By creating a connection between ancient wisdom and modern science, it then becomes possible to reconcile the misunderstandings that have caused numerous unnecessary wars and injustice.

Appendix II—Articles

While the entirety of this manuscript covers too many topics to be absorbed without continual experimentation with reality to verify its contents, a few central topics are relevant enough to warrant publication as stand-alone article without recourse to the underlying theories.

On Food Stamps and Free Markets
by Karun Philip.

While war seems imminent and is occupying the column-inches of newspapers everywhere, the prospects of mass starvation of Afghan civilians should bring to light the important issue of food security for all. Even in India, where PDS godowns are filled with food, there are still people who suffer deprivation and cannot access food. Prime Minister Vajpayee recently announced in the wake of alleged starvation deaths in Orissa, "We are determined to ensure that no one sleeps without food." Well and good, but how exactly can it be done in the most efficient manner?

Both free market capitalism and various flavors of socialism have not succeeded in ensuring good nutrition for everyone. But one system that has worked in the West is food stamps. This is a system by which people below a certain income level get vouchers to buy food from whichever source they choose. The government sets up a fund to reimburse food retailers for presented vouchers. There have been many objections put up to food stamp programs, but given that this has been the only successful system in the world we need to go back to the drawing board and see whether these objections are valid.

"Food stamp systems are liable to fraud and 'scams'"

True enough. But a centrally planned bureaucracy like the PDS is even more liable to fraud. And the arrival of the Internet provides a simple way to prevent fraud—people can register for the food stamp program and have their photographs and details stored digitally. The food vouchers they are issued can have serial numbers, and the shopkeeper accepting the voucher can type in the number on any Internet-connected terminal to check that this voucher was indeed meant for this person. To be sure, people will come up with ways to defraud the system, but with ingenuity and technology we can progress to a virtually unbreakable system, or at least one which can detect fraud after the fact, trace the criminals, and throw them in jail.

"The profit made by the private food retailers and supply chain will increase costs"

On the contrary, competition will do what it always does—constantly innovate and produce ever lower prices. A centrally planned bureaucracy can never decrease the end user-cost because it has no incentive to innovate and no competition to borrow innovations from.

"People will become lazy and de-motivated if they get free food"

This is an absurd argument. In the first place, even if they are such human beings to be satisfied with just food and nothing else, that downside is nothing compared to mass hunger and malnutrition, and the reduction in mental and physical capabilities brought about by poor nutrition. But it is highly unlikely that people will be satisfied with just food, and all it will provide is a sense of security that will allow them to survive the process of globalization which is likely to eliminate their traditional jobs. By providing food security, people will be able to have the courage to go out and learn new skills that will help them earn far more than they could in the pre-modern times.

"Poor countries have no resources to provide food stamps for the massive numbers of poor"

This is true for some countries but not India, where Vajpayee recently announced a Rs. 10,000 crore budget for food security. But even for poorer countries, there is another way to finance a global food stamp program. At my company, we are working on software for what has become the fastest growing innovation in financial services—the securitization of credit. This concept can be used to finance food stamps by giving food stamps as an at-risk loan rather than a grant. Then when people start getting an income beyond some threshold, they would be expected to start repaying the loan. This would be added back to the pool and used to fund new recipients. By pooling these loans, and covering the first, say, 30% of unrecoverable defaults through direct government subsidy or international charity funds, the interest rate on repayment can be adjusted such that the scheme funds itself at affordable interest rates. In addition, the scheme will create a consumer credit database for billions of otherwise ignored people. The knowledge about which of them are conscientious, hard working people who are worthy of credit is very valuable to private enterprises. The conscientious repayers of the food-stamp-loans would spontaneously be rewarded with more credit, more trust, and more opportunity by numerous private sector players. The spin off benefits of this would be huge and would effectively move archaic information-scarce economies to dynamic, data-driven ones practically overnight.

Those who support free markets and globalization need to step forward and admit that it can be combined with a modicum of welfare, as long as the welfare is given as cash-equivalent vouchers or through reinsurance of pools of strategic classes of loans, rather than by controlling prices and strangling free enterprise. Then we will begin to see an end to the violent protests at every single meeting on the subject of globalization and free trade. Then we will see faster and less gut-wrenching economic progress in every country, resulting in win-win growth for all economies. Direct basic welfare is an issue whose critical importance is missed by most economists and sociologists on both sides of the ideological divide today. The idea is simple. The implementation is possible and cheap with the existence of the Internet and information technology. What on earth are we waiting for?

Knowledge Backed Securities

Karun Philip discusses a proposition that taking structured finance to the private skills-training industry can shorten the road back to global prosperity.

In this article I discuss the problems with the economic theory that claims that interest rate cuts will create money supply expansion that will re-start the economy, and then present a way that may help work around these problems.

Whom do we lend to?

On October 2, 2001 the US Federal Reserve cut interest rates once again to a 40-year low of 2.5%. In addition, private money is sitting on cash deposits in large quantities. There is now a large quantity of money in the banking system that economists claim will now be lent cheaply to successful companies, and this will stimulate new jobs and new demand. Great theory, but now look at the state of the successful large companies— they seem to be in no great hurry to borrow because they cannot see anything but decline in demand, and are lowering costs through layoffs, which will reinforce the reduction in consumer demand. There is plenty of capacity in the banking system to lend, but a lack of knowledge of where to lend it profitably and safely. And without growth in lending, there will be no economic growth.

The general consensus is that there will be a period of belt tightening that cannot be avoided. The debate is only whether it will be a short 6-month period, or a decade-long (and counting) experience like Japan's.

Back to school

In every major downturn in the US, people have tended to go back to school during a period where they have been laid off and are finding it difficult to find a new job. If we take a look at this simple wisdom of ordinary people, we can begin to see how an efficient supply of capital to people to retrain themselves with economically valuable skills can be both profitable and sustainable. But instead of looking to college education which is general purpose in nature, we need to look at schools which train people in practical skills—these are the schools that would tend to provide a more predictable return on an investment in training than conventional college degrees. These schools typically provide a large return on capital to their students, but are unable to charge the full value of their training because of the limited purchasing power of their clientele prior to the training.

Loans for training courses

But lending money for training can be a safe and profitable business only if we employ the techniques of structured finance. There can be no guarantee that every student given a loan will be able to get a job of sufficient pay to service the loan. But we *can* collect and analyze data. By forming partnerships with training schools, lenders can build databases on the effectiveness of various types of training, in various parts of the country, and for people of various prior skills. These data sets will lead to the determination of how much default is to be expected, and thereby determine the price of the pool of training loans. The training school will be incented to provide such information since once the data is established and funding becomes available, they may be able to even increase the amount they charge for training, as long as they demonstrate a clear return on investment.

Operational innovations

The innovations from there can be endless. For example:

- Make the training schools hold the equity tranche of the deal so that they are incented to discover ever better ways of making their training more effective.

- Develop ways of credit scoring a training school and its prospective students to ensure that each type of person focuses on the type of career prospects that will maximize their particular aptitude.

- If the training is proven to be sufficiently productive, consolidate older consumer debt such as credit card debt of the borrower into a training loan by lending the cost of training plus the cost of paying off the older debt.

- Discover appropriate training schools for delinquent credit card debtors who can then pay back old debt as well as have the prospect of new earning power after the training investment.

- Provide an online reference check to employers to validate the courses and performance of students who apply for a job. Defaulters and delinquencies can also be flagged on this reference check.

- Provide an online rating of various professions, their average pay, the schools that train for that profession, and the banks that provide financing. This will enable people to find out what skills are most needed in the economy and how to acquire those skills.

Of course the standard tools of structured finance will also be applicable—pools of training loans can be split into waterfalls, interest-only pieces, etc. to tailor the supply of loans to the demand for risk and return in the capital markets.

Macro-economic effects

The data collection needed for building such a 'Knowledge Backed Securities' (KBS) infrastructure into place presents quite a massive task.

But once it is underway, the macro-economic effects of such data being collected and used as a basis for new credit issuance ought to be quite dramatic. Over time, there will be almost endless prospects for investment in areas that are proven to be effective. The greater the pace of technological change, the more will be the need for workers in an economy to upgrade their skill sets multiple times in a career.

The unemployment claims would become virtually zero because everyone would either be in a job, or at a training school (or not seeking work). The training industry could be the source and sink for labor, constantly measuring what types of labor and skills the economy needs, and then supplying that labor before shortages cause bottlenecks on the economy.

Training would become very competitive and only schools that provide the best and most effective training would survive the test of detailed data analysis from Wall Street. However, with the liquidity available for higher investments in training, schools would be able to afford the best salaries in the economy to attract the best talent as teachers. With a way to for those who have useful practical knowledge to monetize that knowledge, the 'habits of highly effective people' will emerge and spread spontaneously as the market seeks out ever more productivity in training.

The massive positive fallout of such a system should be sufficient for the Federal Reserve to encourage KBS to the extent of providing liquidity to AAA-rated KBS, much as it buys rated mortgage products. It could also provide limited reinsurance or lines of credit to pools of loans for the lower end of jobs, where defaults may otherwise be too high.

In general, by investing in market-based training loans, money supply injections from frightened investors or the Federal Reserve can be employed in a way that will rescue consumer credit, and set the stage for demand recovery in a newer, reconfigured economy after bad older investments are written off. The injection of market-monitored training loans into the economy will also stimulate capital investment from businesses that can safely assume that consumer demand will not retreat indefinitely into a shell. While this 'new economy' will continue to be one where no job is safe from redundancy, it can also be one where if one job disappears, many other potential jobs are sure to be around the corner. And if capitalism does its trick of increasing productivity continually, you can bet that the new jobs will afford a higher standard of living than the old ones.

Securitization as Knowledge Management
A proposition that securitization represents the apogee of economic and credit theory; the reasons underlying its ascendancy.

By Karun Philip

The goal of this article is to step back from the day-to-day transactions of the securitization world, and try to locate securitization's place in the financial history of the last 250 years. I will conclude by suggesting that the surge in securitization we are witnessing has been inevitable, and that it will, in fact, continue to expand at an amazing pace over the next couple of decades.

In order to discuss securitization in terms of "knowledge management," we first need a working definition of knowledge. Is it the same as data? The same as information? Or, is it something distinct from these commodities? The problem of what constitutes valid knowledge is at least as old as Socrates.

Fortunately, the 20th century produced some of the most outstanding scientific investigations into knowledge, and the three most significant contributors, in my opinion, are three Viennese: Kurt Gödel, a mathematician, Friedrich Hayek, an economist and Nobel prize winner, and Karl Popper, a philosopher of science.

Hayek and Popper worked closely with each other, and both knew Gödel, though his work was more esoteric.

Gödel's key contribution was the "Incompleteness Theorem," which proved that there is a fundamental obstacle to having all the facts. One is always able to discover missing pieces. Therefore, all "knowledge statements" are necessarily fallible.

Hayek described the way in which societies have historically organized themselves to mitigate fallibility, and derived from that the proposition that socialist central planning will necessarily fail, something no one disputes today.

Popper's many contributions were underlined by a commitment to realization that there is only one objective reality, even though our knowledge about it may or may not be right. He showed how scientific methods, in particular, help to combat fallibility, while remaining imperfect.

The "Vienna Three" and Economic Epistemology

Hayek's observation about historical society was that the key to success was to allow and foster competitive theories. His position was, "Let them battle it out in debate and the most correct ones will survive." This single, brilliant insight led to an entirely new description about how and why economic liberalism worked in Europe and America. He agreed on most major points with Adam Smith, but had a large number of additional contributions about governance, law, and economics.

In his writings on money, Hayek was so far ahead of his contemporaries that no one understood him. Only recently have economists such as Roger Garrison at Auburn University begun to rewrite capital theory taking Hayek's insights into account.

Hayek noted that credit providers compete and thus discover sustainable credit policies. However, Hayek insisted that there is an incentive to oversupply credit and suggested that the solution was to allow competitive currencies. We have all seen the recent global currency activity, which only reinforces this theory that the capital markets will punish currencies that have "crony capitalist" credit regimes.

Practically, however, to have multiple currencies in a single economy at the same time would be impractical because we would have to have prices in multiple currencies. That results in a conflict between money's role as a store of value and as a unit of account.

The problem that Hayek highlights has been a source of contention for the last 250 years. Adam Smith felt that banks should just be left alone and they will resolve their problem. David Hume, while agreeing with many of Smith's other theories, disagreed on this point. His recommendation was bank regulation using a central bank.

Today's public capital markets have shown us a potential alternative that does not require multiple units of account. We shall now discuss further and see how it approximates Hayek's monetary competition.

We must note here that Hayek is making us see credit as knowledge. In practical terms: we can look at loan performance data over diverse samples and use data mining to find types of enterprises that will succeed. Technically, this conversion of data to knowledge is a process called "induction," i.e., development of a general principle from the available data.

We must bear in mind that, though evidence mitigates fallibility, it does not eliminate it. One day you may think from data that inverse floaters are risk free, and the next day you may find that they blow up because something unexpected happens—an inversion of the yield curve, perhaps—and fills in some incompleteness in your former argument.

The best we can do, synthesizing Hayek and Popper, is ensure that any decision to go with a specific theory looks at three aspects.

The first would be to examine the circumstances on a deductive basis , e.g., that inverse floaters will behave in a certain way provided all players have rational expectations

Further, one needs to consider the evidence; there should be other people who have done it before. Of course, those who are risk-taking innovators must necessarily ignore this caveat.

Finally, the prospective course of action or decision should be able to survive argument, debate, and critique by a number of individuals with multiple perspectives.

Securitization: Perfection of Credit

Before we specifically address securitized credit in this context, we need to re-think our conception of credit.

Instead of viewing credit as backed by deposit liabilities in a bank, we need to start thinking about the collateral (or business model) that underlies each loan. Then for each type of asset and each industry, we can collect industry specific data and this data will guide our decisions.

Once we have these pools of data, we can manage risk by pooling these asset-backed loans and creating fungible bonds, i.e., bonds that are not associated with particular loans in the pool but a fraction of the entire pool.

In this structure, deduction via the asset type and business model, and induction through data, reduce fallibility. The remaining risk is further reduced by the pooling process. We can now estimate the degree of losses in the pool without needing to know which exact loan will default, and cover the expected losses using the appropriate interest rates.

Securitization started as a balance sheet management strategy. Banks had loans and wanted to get them off balance sheet to release capital to fund new loans.

Today, securitization applications are headed in the reverse direction. Bankers are looking at the demand for different types of assets in the securitization market and then making the credit decision.

This brings the competitive debate and critique of thousands of market players into the equation. Asset backed bond prices represent an "intertemporal" consensus on the relative risk of lending in that sector. The individual loan officer has access to the knowledge of those thousands of players simply by looking at a price.

The process of bringing science and engineering to banking proceeds by increasing complexity in the quantification of credit. In the face of inevitable fallibility of knowledge, there is one maxim that has worked fairly consistently for a long time: the law of large numbers. When we have multiple loans in a pool, we are fairly accurate in being able to model prepayment speeds, default rates, and so on. But we need a pool to accomplish this; one data point cannot be statistically modeled.

The market has also tended to aggregate similar asset types into a pool, and split up the pool on the abstracted financial risk type—prepayments, defaults, interest rate volatility, currency risk, country risk, etc. An essential part of such modeling is to stress test underlying assumptions.

Already, the market is beginning to develop a vocabulary that captures the risk management and knowledge management aspect of securitization. "Structured finance" is used as a collective term for these techniques, whereby we need not create and sell securities, but can simply retain them on the balance sheet.

Essentially, "structured finance" represents the application of engineering discipline and techniques to the art of finance. It is founded on massive use of data and modeling (rather than the fallible discretion of loan officers in banks). It has involved subjecting models to the test of reality. And, it has resulted in designing and tailoring risk so that risk supply (the loans in the market) is matched with risk demand (the investor appetite for risk and return). This transformation of risk is the essence of a structured finance deal.

If we step back a little and take a look at the macro trends, there seems to be an irreversible shift occurring at the current time.

The old model of banking, in Adam Smith and David Hume's time, involved a two-step process. Savers would deposit money in the bank (which formed the bank's liabilities on its balance sheet) and then banks would make loans to enterprises. The new model has collapsed that into a single step: banks make loans that are securitized into pools and tranches off the pool are sold to depositors. Of course, the depositor may use intermediaries such as pension funds, hedge funds, and mutual funds.

In the extreme case, cash (i.e., demand deposits) becomes obsolete. All money is held in named securities of the choice of the holder. Those securities would have fully disclosed underlying asset performance data, so the depositor knows the exact exposure to risk.

Small investors need not fear this because it is fairly easy for a bank to create a safe security as long as the buyer is willing to accept a return that is below the average return on capital in the economy. Larger investors would have managed risk portfolios. The David Hume problem of systemic bank collapses would become impossible.

If we achieve depositor protection, can we expect that Austrian economists theories of free banking will now emerge?

In my opinion, the answer is "yes." As automation and the use of the Internet increases, we could move to a system where each individual manages his own risk portfolio.

With free banking, Adam Smith's desire for unlimited banking would be realized, but only in a way that meets David Hume's objection. The natural limits of free banking in this regime would be that banks can lend as much as they want but only if there is a market to buy those loans. This would keep a spontaneous check on the quality of money, as was envisaged by Hayek's competitive currency regime, without actually needing such a regime.

What are the implications for the current players in the securitization industry? Here are my impressions.

We must be prepared for massive growth. Sure, the industry is growing at $200 billion a year and that feels pretty good. But we are still at the bottom of the S-curve of growth. We should expect that in the next 10 to 20 years, we will complete the transition to virtually 100 percent securitization of all forms of credit, if we include CBO/CLO deals and future innovations we have yet to see.

The biggest impediment to such a vision of the future is transaction costs. Today it is not viable to do a small deal, although the risk management benefits would accrue whether the deal is small or large. At Tranquilmoney, we have been working on complete automation using Net-based technologies, and have successfully managed transactions as small as a $30 pharmacy receivable that turns in 30 days. In addition, we need technologies to integrate portfolio reporting with loan servicing so that data accuracy is guaranteed.

For institutions already involved in this field, we need to prepare for growth in both volume and complexity. This would mean investment in analytics and research, in educating the depositor, including smaller depositors in the future when regulations are eased. We must get used to the fact that securitization is here to stay, and those that ignore this tidal wave of change do so at their own peril.

BIBLIOGRAPHY

Aristotle, Menger, Mises: An Essay in the Metaphysics of Economics, by Barry Smith.
http://wings.buffalo.edu/philosophy/faculty/smith/articles/menger.html.

Conjecture and Refutation, by Karl Popper

Eric Lott on Sri Ramanuja.
http://www.rediff.com/news/1999/nov/01inter.htm.

Free Banking and Monetary Reform, by David Glasner.

From Dawn To Decadence, by Jacques Barzun.

Good Money, Volumes 1 & 2, by F. A. Hayek.

Human Action, by Ludwig von Mises.

In Defense of Extreme (Fallibilistic) Apriorism, by Barry Smith.
http://wings.buffalo.edu/philosophy/faculty/smith/articles/ROTH-BARD.htm.

The Affluent Society, by J. K. Galbraith.

The Anatomy of Power, by J. K. Galbraith.

The Constitution of Liberty, by F. A. Hayek.

The Fatal Conceit, by F. A. Hayek.

The Hayek-L list managed by Greg Ransom at http://www.hayekcenter.org with archives available at http://maelstrom.stjohns.edu/archives/hayek-l.html.

The Road To Serfdom, by F. A. Hayek.

The Sensory Order, by F. A. Hayek.

The Implications of Gödel's Theorem, by J. R. Lucas. http://users.ox.ac.uk/~jrlucas/implic.html.

Law, Legislation & Liberty, by F. A. Hayek.

Reviews, papers and articles on Popper, by Rafe Champion. http://zap.to/rafechampion.

Tranquilmoney—an online software platform for financial engineering and management of securitization deals. Co-founded by Karun Philip. http://www.tranquilmoney.com.